Sto V

REBEL ON TWO CONTINENTS
Thomas Meagher

Born: August 23, 1823
Died: June 29, 1867

Great Irish patriot, exiled rebel, fighting Union general and Governor of the wild Montana Territory, Thomas Meagher packed many lifetimes' adventure and achievement into one incredible career. He was a man who refused to put power above principle, and his story continues to be relevant and meaningful in a world where the fight for man's freedom and dignity has never ended.

BOOKS BY DAVID J. ABODAHER

FREEDOM FIGHTER
  Casimir Pulaski

REBEL ON TWO CONTINENTS
  Thomas Meagher

WARRIOR ON TWO CONTINENTS
  Thaddeus Kosciuszko

Rebel on Two Continents

THOMAS MEAGHER

by DAVID J. ABODAHER

JULIAN
MESSNER

NEW YORK

Published simultaneously in the United States and Canada
by Julian Messner, a division of Simon & Schuster, Inc.,
1 West 39 Street, New York, N.Y. 10018. All rights reserved.

For
DAVID J. GILLESPIE
American-Irish
in the mold of Meagher

Printed in the United States of America

ISBN 0-671-32355-5 Cloth Trade
0-671-32356-3 MCE

Library of Congress Catalog Card No. 70-123168

CONTENTS

I

A SEED IS PLANTED

Eleven-year-old Tom Meagher had climbed Mount Misery many times before. Until this sunny, hot afternoon in late August 1834, his heart always had been warmed by the view from the crest of the high hill. He had sat there so often, thrilled by the beauty. Surely, he had thought, there could be no more wonderful place in all the wide world than Ireland.

Below him, not far from the foot of the mountain, were the clear waters of the Suir River, flowing peaceably through Waterford, the village in which he was born. In the past he had let his eyes scan the Irish countryside, first searching for the bridge over the Suir. Beyond he would see the rooftop of the comfortable Meagher home, the other neat houses nearby and the church spires piercing the cloudless sky. Then, following the sparkling waters of the Suir, he would admire the broad bay that formed Waterford Harbour on Ireland's southeast coast.

Not far west were the blue-green peaks of the Comeragh Mountains.

Today, Tom Meagher saw none of the beauty. He sat, for the first time, wondering if Mount Misery had been named for the poor, hungry people of Waterford. He knew, of course, that some people had more wealth than others. His father, manager of a prosperous shipping business owned by the Meagher family, was considered well-to-do. But to have so little that there was nothing to eat was unthinkable. Until that morning.

Tom had accompanied his father to the quay, the Waterford docks. He was to leave later in the week to begin his studies at Clongowes-Wood, a Jesuit college in County Kildare, near Dublin, about seventy-five miles north. Very close to his father—his mother had died when he was a boy—Tom wished to be with him whenever possible his last few days in Waterford.

On the quay one of the Meagher ships was ready to weigh anchor and sail for America. The ship's deck teemed with men, women and young children. Many of the faces were familiar to Tom. He recognized first one, then others, who had been long-time residents of the village. He saw unhappiness on their faces, deep sorrow in eyes filled with tears.

"Why are they so sad, Papa?" Tom asked his father. "Going on holiday, shouldn't they be happy?"

"Theirs is no holiday, lad," the elder Thomas Meagher answered in a hushed voice. "They leave their homes for America, and they are sad to leave the Ireland they love, as we do, knowing they may never again come back."

"But why, if they love Ireland, must they leave?"

"Because, lad, they face only starvation here. With no jobs for the men, and no food for the children, they despair. They feel a little hope in a new land. Many go to America. Some to Canada. Others to Australia. Anywhere to escape."

"Escape what, Papa?"

"Persecution, my son," Thomas Meagher replied.

Tom, who knew more than a little of Irish history, understood what his father meant. He remembered stories he had heard of the English domination of Ireland which began in the twelfth century, and of Edward Bruce, who helped organize the resistance against British rule in the fourteenth century. But that had been long before.

"But we have our own representatives in Parliament, Papa. Can't they make laws for the good of Ireland?"

"They should, son," Thomas Meagher said. "But too often the Parliamentarians represent only the rich landowners and not the people. Hence laws are made to favor England, not Ireland."

Tom frowned. "How can such things be?"

His father shook his head. "It is a sad thing, Tom," he said. "But when men fear they may lose something, they often become traitors to their own kind. Many of our own lawmakers have been bought by England and pass laws to please our conquerors."

Tom thought for a moment. "Is King William such a bad man that he does not want the Irish people to have food?" he asked finally.

"The King does only what he thinks is best for England and for him. Until the King and the English Parliament recognize the right of Ireland to be free, the persecution will go on. The Irish will die of starvation. Some will leave for other lands. And Ireland will grow weaker and England's hold will become stronger."

"Why does one people persecute another, Papa, when Jesus taught us that all men are equal and we should love one another?" Tom asked.

Thomas Meagher's brow knotted. "How can I explain it to you, my son?" he said. "Mostly it must be fear. Fear of the unknown. Fear of what is different and what they do not understand."

"But, Papa, why does this make them so cruel and heartless?"

Tom's father shrugged his shoulders. "Good men have searched for the answer to that since the beginning of the world," he said sadly. "Maybe it has no end, this distrust of men of one country or one race or one religion for those who are not like themselves. Perhaps they believe it is a self-defense to fight and destroy."

"But why should England wish to destroy Ireland?"

"No, no, lad," Thomas Meagher protested. "England does not want to destroy Ireland, merely to control it. Why is that? Because, like most nations, England wants to grow, to become more powerful. It has a tight hold on us now and will not give us up without much fighting and bloodshed."

"As they did with the colonies in America?"

His father nodded. "Perhaps that's why England treats

us so badly now. Losing the colonies was a great blow to a country which considers itself one of the most powerful in the world. It may be that they fight harder to hold Ireland because of their damaged pride."

The elder Meagher thought for a moment, then continued, "But, Tom, you must not think that it is only we Irish who suffer. All through the world there is persecution and grabbing of land by foreign countries. Poland is besieged by not one but three—Russia, Germany and Austria all are stealing Polish territory. But the greatest, most heartless persecution and the longest is that of the Jews. For centuries they've had no country of their own and are driven away wherever they settle or forced to live apart in ghettos. All because their beliefs are different."

His father's words filtered through Tom's memory as he sat atop Mount Misery, high above Waterford. He understood more now. He even knew why one of his playmates, weeks before, had called him a "dirty papist."

It was as though Tom Meagher's eyes had been suddenly opened. He had looked on poverty before, but had never really seen it. He had listened to tales of Irish history, and stories of Irish patriots dying for their home land, but hadn't actually heard them or recognized their significance.

Tom Meagher had always loved Ireland, but until that afternoon on Mount Misery, his love had meant hardly more than just a word to speak. Now, understanding the reality of oppression and misrule, seeing the effects of poverty and suffering, his love began flowering into a passion. He would go gladly to Clongowes-Wood. He would study hard, grow up, learn all he needed to help in the fight for Irish freedom.

Thomas Francis Meagher was born on August 23, 1823, as Ireland approached the peak of its suffering centuries. At one time that great, beautiful green island in the northeast Atlantic had been ruled only by Irish kings. Irishmen had owned their own lands, worked their own farms. Ireland, then—in the late 700's—was a leading center of European culture.

In the year A.D. 795 the Viking Norsemen began to invade Ireland. They took over the coast first, seizing the cities of Dublin, Limerick and Waterford, and then moved inland. For over two centuries the Vikings dominated the island. It was not until the year 1014, when Brian Boru, one of Ireland's greatest kings, defeated a Norse alliance at the battle of Clontarf, that Ireland was free for a time, and the Irish again owned their own land.

For a century and a half Ireland was peacefully Irish. Then, in 1155 Pope Adrian IV gave Ireland to King Henry II of England on condition that he put the Irish church in order. The authority by which the Pope could give a country and its people to a foreign king remains one of history's great puzzles. In 1166 England began its invasion of Ireland.

The English forced their way across the green island with strength. Backed up by powerful armies, they gave the Irish little chance to fight back. Whatever resistance there was came mostly from the southern areas. Ulster, the northern part of Ireland, accepted English rule with only token uprisings.

King Henry divided Irish lands among his favored English noblemen. Those who actually owned the farms were allowed to live on the property if they worked the land profitably, the profits to go to the English absentee landowners. For almost seven hundred years the Irish found it impossible to escape from English domination, though again and again Irish patriots would emerge from hiding to lead ill-fated rebellions. After the Reformation, when England turned Protestant, tyranny became identified more and more in the Irish mind with the reformed religion. It became a kind of patriotism—often the only defiance an Irishman could offer—to cling to the older church. Ireland grew staunchly Catholic.

Perhaps the most devastating English assault against the Irish was the result of Oliver Cromwell's arrival on Irish soil. Invading Ireland to quell another uprising, he settled many of his soldiers on Irish land, driving the Catholics to the western reaches of the island. This was in 1649 when Cromwell's campaign broke the back of Irish resistance.

Hatred for Englishmen smouldered under the surface, for there was little the Irish Catholics could do openly. Though England finally allowed the Irish their own Parliament late in the eighteenth century, she made certain of the Protestant ascendancy—that the only Irish serving in the legislative body were Protestants. Even these could do little to help Ireland, subject, as they were, to English overlordship.

Severe penal laws were passed that further hamstrung Irish progress. The middle classes, and these were principally Catholic, were excluded from the trades and professions. Everything was done that could be done to render the Catholic majority helpless to rise against England.

Ireland's population, numbering 4.5 million in the late 1700's, included more than three million Catholics. With few exceptions, they were the peasants and laborers, unable to own land or better their lot because of English suppression. England's policy of having her subject-peoples make money for the home treasury, the same policy which brought rebellion in America, brought ruin to Ireland.

Tenant farmers, paying high rents to English landlords, had little money left for food and necessities. They were forced to depend on the potato for subsistence. Their difficulties meant financial trouble for others.

Fishermen along the extensive Irish coasts could not sell their fish because those who had been their best customers had no money with which to buy. And, taking in no money themselves, the fishermen could not buy salt with which to salt down and preserve their catches. Other businesses, even those controlled by Protestant upper classes, suffered. These included the brewing, distilling, cotton and linen industries.

In 1798 Protestants began to join Catholics in protesting the injustices. A Catholic-Protestant coalition, led by Wolfe Tone, revolted openly. This uprising, poorly organized as were all the others, was quickly quashed. The English Parliament, concerned now that Protestants and

Catholics were joining together in protest, quickly passed the Act of Union—a law which all but nullified the Irish Parliament.

The faithful Irish protested more loudly. Street fights ensued. The result was only more bloodshed, tighter controls and increased poverty. There was no hope for any man of ambition in Ireland.

Frustrated by this lack of opportunity, Tom Meagher's grandfather left Ireland for Newfoundland in the early 1800's. There he built a prosperous shipping business. Planning to expand his shipping interests between Newfoundland and Ireland, Grandfather Meagher sent his son Thomas back to Ireland as manager.

So it was that Thomas Meagher settled in Waterford and married, and young Tom Meagher was born in Ireland, not in the New World. Tall, lean, handsome and bright-eyed, Tom Meagher attended the best school in Waterford. He was a good student and popular with his classmates, aggressive and articulate even as a boy.

Tom left Waterford that August 1834 to enter the Jesuit college at Clongowes-Wood. He was immediately thrilled by the beauty of the setting as he walked slowly up the tree-lined path toward the ancient castle in which the college was housed. The great battlemented towers which marked the corners of the huge masonry building excited his imagination. Sitting at the crest of a hill and surrounded by densely forested areas, it was an inspiring sight. Tom wondered how much of Ireland's tragic history the massive structure might have witnessed. He soon learned.

Late the afternoon of his first day at Clongowes-Wood, Tom was taken around the castle by Father Michael Callahan, one of his instructors.

"Tread softly, my boy," the priest said as they walked through the spacious, cobbled entrance hall. "The spirits of brave men who gave their blood for Ireland hover about these walls."

"What do you mean, Father?" Tom asked.

"It was less than two hundred years ago," Father Callahan answered, "in 1649, Master Meagher. Oliver Cromwell came that year from England to grind Ireland further under the British heel. There was a bold and brave defense of the families who sought refuge in the castle here, made right where you stand."

"What happened, Father Callahan?"

"It is sad, my son," the priest said mournfully. "Sad and grim. Cromwell's legions were too much for our poorly armed defenders. The tragic thing is they were shown no mercy, even though they were promised clemency when the castle fell."

"What happened to the people?"

"Cromwell's soldiers took them all, men, women and children, to Dublin, driving them cruelly on foot all the way. There all the men were hanged, and the women and children also murdered. May God rest their martyred souls."

"And may Cromwell and his raiders be rotting in hell!" Tom exploded.

"Hush, lad!" the priest admonished. "Let us not

nourish the same hate. God has no doubt punished them long since." He shook his head. "Terrible, terrible! So great was the ruin and the devastation, so many Irishmen were slaughtered like cattle by Cromwell's Puritan army, that when autumn came hardly anyone remained to harvest the crops."

Father Callahan's words kept whirling through Tom's head as he tried to sleep that night. He twisted and turned, wishing again and again that he was already old enough to do something for Ireland. He resolved to study hard and complete his education as soon as possible. Meanwhile he would learn everything he could about Irish history, about the injustices and what caused them.

Names began to float through his memory. Names of people he had heard mentioned by his father and his friends, men he'd have to learn more about. There was Henry Grattan for one. He had fought and finally succeeded in freeing the Irish Parliament from English government control in 1782, if only for a time. Grattan had also gained, in 1792, the right for Catholics to vote. He had even achieved the right for them to sit in Parliament. George III had overruled Catholic membership in Parliament in 1798, and Tom now remembered that the King's action had led to another bloody revolt called the Rising of 1798.

There was also Wolfe Tone, another Irish patriot who took part in that rising. Wolfe Tone had argued for French help and had received some. He led several expeditions into Ireland but was always forced back to

France. Then, during the Rising of '98, he was again defeated by the English and, this time, captured. In despair, Tone had killed himself.

He could not, of course, overlook Daniel O'Connell, who was even then carrying on the fight for Irish freedom. Tom was vaguely aware of the powerful Catholic Association which O'Connell founded. The association, under O'Connell's leadership, had so stirred things that England allowed passage of the Catholic Emancipation Act in 1829. Tom knew that O'Connell's great fight of the moment was repeal of the Union with England and solution of the land question which throttled Irish progress.

Beginning the next day, Tom Meagher spent almost all his free hours in the Clongowes-Wood library. He searched first for an understanding of the problem of Irish land ownership which had reached a crisis about that time. Uncertain of the meaning of what he read, he turned to Father Callahan.

"It is much too complex a subject for so young a mind, Master Meagher," the priest told him.

"But I must understand it, Father," Tom insisted. "I must."

"It will take much study, Tom," Father Callahan warned. "But let me try to start you off. The problem goes back many centuries. About seven hundred years ago the feudal landholding system was first imposed on Ireland, though feudalism had existed in other lands long before."

Tom had already learned that the feudal system had

begun with the sweep west from China by the Huns, who lived off the countries they conquered and ravished. It became common throughout Europe when the Germanic tribes started the many migrations that destroyed the Roman Empire.

"In feudalism," Father Callahan explained, "ownership of all land is vested in the king of the controlling country. He delegates pieces of that land to certain chosen high nobles, who, in turn, assign some of it to lesser nobles. The nobility and knighthood provided protection and housing for the peasants and serfs, and the peasants supported them by working the land."

"It's not fair!" Tom exclaimed. "The ones who do the work get little. And Irish land is not owned by Irishmen, and Irishmen have no say in its use!"

"True on all counts, lad."

"Was Ireland never master of its own territory, Father?" Tom asked.

The priest nodded. "For perhaps a century and a half after Brian Boru drove out the Vikings," he said. "There was no foreign interference then. But when Pope Adrian IV made England's King Henry II overlord of Ireland, our troubles began. First the Tudors confiscated Irish property and took it for their own. Then Cromwell and his Puritans all but stripped us clean, and almost all that remained William III appropriated."

"Is not Daniel O'Connell now speaking out against English ownership of Irish land?" Tom asked.

"That he is, Tom," Father Callahan said. "He is our hope of today, making the fire that keeps our torch of freedom burning. There is an old book in the library containing his best speeches, including those which spurred the passage of the Catholic Emancipation Act. As one of my debating team, it would help you to read them, to learn the passion in words which influence men to your thinking."

Tom found the old book. It was dog-eared, almost in rags. He read, then reread O'Connell's speeches, again and again, holding the book carefully, turning the pages cautiously.

"I do not want to destroy it further," he told Father Callahan. "I love it the more because it is so tattered. It shows how many have read the great man's words."

"You have a perceptive mind, Tom," the priest complimented him. "For if so many have read O'Connell, it means there is yet hope for Ireland, since they must have found inspiration there."

O'Connell's fiery speeches did more than excite Tom Meagher's imagination. They gave added importance to his debating classes, for the more he read the more determined he became to develop himself into as fine an orator as Daniel O'Connell. When his school days were finished, he promised himself, he would travel Ireland, speaking out against the injustices being done to his native land.

Tom's growing passion to become a public speaker in the image of Daniel O'Connell made his years at Clongowes-Wood pass happily and quickly. Impatient to begin helping his beloved Ireland, he worked hard, almost obsessively, to perfect his platform technique. By the time his sixth, and last, year at the college neared its end, he was already acclaimed the finest public speaker ever to attend the school.

His father came north for the graduation ceremonies, sitting in the audience bursting with pride. Tom's friendly, outgoing personality and infectious sense of humor had earned him the respect and affection of most of his classmates. Thomas Meagher, seeing his son applauded warmly by the other members of the graduating class as he carried away honor after honor, continually dabbed at his tear-filled eyes with a handkerchief.

When it was all over, it was time to leave Clongowes-Wood. Father Michael Callahan brought Tom Meagher down to his emotionally charged father.

"I give him into your charge, Mr. Meagher," Father Callahan said. "Never in my many years at Clongowes-Wood have I seen a boy who has worked more diligently and grown to manhood so quickly. You must be very proud of your lad."

"I am," Thomas Meagher exclaimed, his voice choked. "I am indeed." He drew Tom close and embraced him. "Ah, lad," he said in a whisper, "if your mother, God rest her, were only here today!"

Father Callahan, not wanting to intrude on the emotional scene between father and son, had turned to look up at the sky. After a moment he turned back to Tom and his father.

"And what will the future be for Ireland's young hope?" he asked.

Thomas Meagher's eyes glistened bright. "The law!" he exclaimed. "What else for one with so silver a tongue. How about that, lad?"

"Perhaps, Father," Tom answered.

"Perhaps, he says!" Thomas Meagher laughed. "Let it be so. There is time. First, there is more school to be had. And a knowledge of the world outside Ireland. Stonyhurst! How about that?"

"Stonyhurst!" Tom exploded. "But that is in England!"

"Where else?" Thomas Meagher said. "To help Ireland, one must know its enemy. How better than to finish your schooling in their midst."

"It's a fine college, Stonyhurst," Father Callahan put in. "Your father is very wise, Tom. And Stonyhurst is Catholic, remember. Taught by the Jesuits."

Tom smiled. "Very well," he said. "Stonyhurst it will be."

II
ARROW IN FLIGHT

Tom Meagher spent the summer of 1841 at home in Waterford. It was a busy time, as he prepared himself for the trip across the Irish Sea to England and Stonyhurst College. The first weeks were happy ones, greeting friends and, whenever he could, climbing Mount Misery to dream and plan. As he had done so often before, he would sit there on the crest of the hill, looking far out across the blue of the ocean to where it merged into the azure of the sky.

This morning early in August, just two weeks before his eighteenth birthday, he was made suddenly aware that even greater tragedy than he suspected was crippling Ireland. Walking back from early Mass, he had seen a funeral procession making its way toward the church. No unusual sight except, the thought struck him, this was the fourth in four days in Waterford. He mentioned the fact to his father.

"I can see you are happy to be home, son," Thomas

Meagher told him, "and I am also happy that you are here for even so short a time. So I could not spoil your vacation. Bad trouble has struck the land, for the poor even worse than the worst the English could do." Thomas Meagher looked for a moment into Tom's eyes. "Besides," he went on, "you are much too serious for a young lad, as Father Callahan told you. Be happy that you may study with a clear mind. Enjoy the pleasures and games that boys find joy in doing."

"I will be eighteen soon, Father," Tom said. "A boy no longer, but a man. So what is this great trouble? I must know."

"Have you not seen, Tom, that the food on even our table has been less than before?" Thomas Meagher asked. He then went on to explain.

Tom stood listening without interruption, clenching and unclenching his fists as his father's words sank into his mind. He left the house in silence after his father finished and made his way to Mount Misery. He sat facing not the sea, but to the north, contemplating the lush green of the island and the sparkle of the many lakes. So beautiful a land, he thought—certainly God would not let it go to ruin. Yet, it must have been God Himself who willed this new nightmare for Ireland.

The pratie, as the Irish called the potato, had for centuries been the mainstay of the Irish diet, especially among the poor. Without the pratie, the average Irishman faced starvation. Only the wealthy favored by the English could afford what little meat was to be had, for almost all livestock, cattle and sheep was exported to

England. So, too, with grain, the scanty wheat crop and the flax from which fine Irish linen was made.

The potato blight had started slowly in the spring of 1840, the plants in central Ireland attacked by the devastating black-and-yellow striped beetle. Within the year the killing insects had swept north, south, east and west. Although the potato blight did not reach its peak until between 1845 and 1847, when hundreds of thousands died, few edible potatoes were to be found between Donegal and Waterford by early summer of 1841. Starvation followed. Disease struck. The Irish poor died. And there was no immediate hope in sight.

Tom looked out from his perch atop Mount Misery, wondering. The English could not be blamed for the potato blight. But the hundreds, perhaps thousands, who had already died of starvation, and the many thousands of deaths likely to come, certainly they must be laid at England's doorstep. Ireland produced enough food to feed its people if only it could remain in Ireland. But rich Irish landowners, kept in positions of power by the absentee-landlord system, sold most of their produce abroad.

Ireland, predominantly Catholic, had ceased to have any rights when England established the Church of Ireland—Anglican—as the state religion. England denied Irish Catholics the right to practice their religion, imprisoned priests and treated them no better than robbers and murderers. As if that weren't enough, England levied heavy taxes on Irish Catholics to support the English Church. Perhaps England expected Ireland to be grateful that many Catholic schools in both countries were left undisturbed.

The Americans, chafing under far fewer tyrannies than Ireland suffered, revolted only once and in a few years achieved their independence of England. Ireland had been subjected to English domination for centuries, had revolted again and again, yet was still under Britain's heel and suffering more than ever. Tom wondered what difference there was between the successful uprising of the American colonies and the many risings in Ireland, all of which had ended in failure. He resolved to study both, to find an answer, once he reached Stonyhurst.

Stonyhurst, still a famous Jesuit college, sat low in a lush green valley framed by high, sloping hills. The massive stone building marked by a pair of tall towers, each of which was crested with a large stone eagle, had a setting, Tom thought, as beautiful as that of Clongowes-Wood. Dense forests surrounded three sides of the building and four narrow rivers rippled their way between the stately trees.

Tom took an immediate liking to his prefect, Father William Johnson. "Father is so gentle and kind a man," he wrote his father. "He has the softest whisper for a voice. Boys who have been here one and two years say they would die for him."

Father Johnson, understanding and compassionate, noticed almost at once the deep intensity of Tom Meagher's nature. There was repressed fire in the young man which needed an outlet before it reached tragic explosiveness. He probed carefully for the reason but without success. Tom, realizing he was in England, the home base of Ireland's enemy, was cautious. He was there only to learn, not fight. Time enough for that after he returned to Irish ground.

The priest, however, was determined to ease Tom's mind away from whatever disturbed him. One sure way, he thought, was to have the boy concentrate on a difficult task. Tom's thorough Irish background gave him the opportunity.

"Thomas, my boy," Father Johnson said one day, "I hear you have great ambitions to become a public speaker of note."

"Yes, Father, and is it wrong, since I wish to become a lawyer?" Tom answered, his tone more than a little edgy.

"Easy, lad," the priest said softly. "I mean only to help, for it is a fine calling, and I have reports from Father Edward, your debate instructor, that you already have the silver tongue of an Edmund Burke."

"Edmund Burke?"

"You've not heard of Burke?" Father Johnson smiled. "And you an Irishman!"

Tom shrugged his shoulders. "Daniel O'Connell is the greatest of the Irish speakers," he said sharply.

"True," the priest agreed, looking into Tom's eyes with a warm and disarming smile. He felt, for the first time, that he was nearing the answer to the riddle of the young man's pent-up anger. "Edmund Burke was born in Dublin, but came to England and was—almost fifty years ago—one of the honorable and outspoken members of Parliament."

"Then he was more England's than Ireland's."

"No, Thomas. It would be unjust to so label Edmund Burke. He was a man who fought for justice for humanity as—tell me if I am wrong—it is in your heart to do."

Tom ignored the inference, though Father Johnson noticed he did not say he was wrong. "I know nothing of Edmund Burke," he said simply.

"You surely know of the colonies across the Atlantic and their revolt at being taxed without representation?"

Tom nodded. "And they won their independence and are now their own masters," he said.

Father Johnson did not miss the edge in Tom's voice. To ease the boy's tension he said prayerfully: "As we hope will soon be the good fortune of Ireland."

Tom looked up, puzzled, a little embarrassed. "What did Burke do to help the colonies?"

"Who knows whether he helped or not?" the priest answered. "The point is, Burke was a man of courage in Parliament. He said what he believed, even though it was contrary to general acceptance. He saw the injustices being done the colonies and continually spoke out against them, as your Daniel O'Connell has done. Someday—who knows when—his honesty and bravery will also bear fruit."

"But you are English, Father Johnson," Tom said, surprised by the frankness of the priest.

"Thomas, Thomas," the priest remonstrated, "do you

think all Englishmen condone injustice merely because our leaders allow greed, rather than humanity, to dictate their actions?" He paused, then spoke again. "But I had other reasons for speaking of your ambitions. You know I am also the instructor in the drama, among my other duties?" When Tom nodded, he continued: "It would help you very much in your work with the law and in public speaking to be part of my little actors' group. And you will also get much pleasure from it."

Tom Meagher became one of Father Johnson's budding thespians and almost immediately a tug-of-war developed between Tom and the priest. Tom was so thoroughly Irish he had a brogue "thick as an oak-tree trunk," as Father Johnson expressed it. A language purist, the priest was determined that Tom would lose the accent. But Tom, fiercely loyal to his people and proud of his Irish heritage, considered his speech a badge of honor, not to be tampered with.

The group had been working for two months, rehearsing Shakespeare's *Much Ado About Nothing*. Tom had been assigned the role of Don Pedro, Prince of Arragon, and this day, as they progressed through Act IV, Father Johnson allowed Tom to have his way. It had been a mistake, but the priest bit his lip and suffered the heavy brogue through the early action.

Then came Hero's denial that anyone spoke with her outside her chamber window the night before, followed by Don Pedro's specific charges. Tom, as Don Pedro, addressed Leonato, Governor of Messina, in his richest brogue.

"Enough!" Father Johnson called out. "Master Meagher, I have never heard such a slaughter of the king's English! That brogue—surely—there must be—"

"I am sorry, Father," Tom said with a straight face. "But I was born with it and, God willing, will die with it. But I think it's much ado about nothing you are making of it."

The class broke up in loud guffaws at Tom's play on words. For a few moments Father Johnson's face flamed with anger, but soon he, too, joined in the laughter.

"Well, well," he said when order had finally been restored, "after all, this is playacting. And you have acted the Irishman well, Thomas. Perhaps before you leave Stonyhurst in two years the cheese"—and he pronounced "cheese" as Tom would have said it—"will have melted off your tongue. At least we can pray for that happy day. Class dismissed."

Though he felt continually tense, as if he were under the enemy's gun and had to watch his every word and action, Tom found great pleasure at Stonyhurst. Brogue or no, his professors were convinced he was destined to be a great orator. Dedicated to a cause, he was a brilliant student whatever the subject. Even in his play he held nothing back.

On the cricket team, no player was more aggressive at the wicket than Tom. He was equally erratic.

"Easy, Meagher! Easy!" a teammate would shout. "Face it, you'll never be a William Clark or a Fuller Pilch," referring to two of the greatest cricket players of the time.

It was Rugby football, however, that gave Tom

Meagher the most effective release for his pent-up anti-English aggression. It was rough-and-tumble, with twenty on a side making forty in all on the field. Tom especially enjoyed the fierce scrummaging, somewhat different from the scrimmage of American football.

Scrummaging in Rugby found most of the forty players locked and wedged together in a heaving mass for as long as ten minutes and more at a time. Each of the men would struggle and kick for a ball which few of them could see. This naturally resulted in a number of shins being barked accidentally.

Accidental kicking evolved into intentional kicking, called hacking—a deliberate, and in those days legal, means of forcing one's way through the opposition. "Hacking over," kicking the shins of a player when running, was another recognized form of it. Tom Meagher could give and take hacks with the best of them.

Early during his last year at Stonyhurst, Tom received good news from home, news that seemed to promise great hope for Ireland's future. For two hundred years English laws had prohibited the election of any Catholic to the mayoralty of any Irish village or city. With the prejudicial law relaxed, Tom's own father, Thomas Meagher, had been elected mayor of Waterford.

Tom was jubilant. His fourth year at Stonyhurst could not end soon enough. He returned home in the early summer of 1843, a determined young man of almost twenty years.

III
OPPORTUNITY MAKES A MAN

Tom had barely arrived in Waterford before his hopes for Ireland sank. The change in the election laws which allowed his Catholic father to become mayor of Waterford was hardly more than a crumb tossed by the English. Nothing had been done to ease the famine and starvation.

The responsibility of his office combined with the agony and suffering of the citizens of Waterford had sapped Thomas Meagher's strength. Tom saw how much his father had aged and this too tore at his heart. Something had to be done. But what?

Thomas Meagher, in turn, was greatly concerned for his son. He had finished his studies at Stonyhurst with high honors. Tom, he was resolved, had to continue his studies, whether at an Irish or English university. Tom had other ideas.

"It is out of the question, Father," Tom said. "The cost is too great. It is time I earned my keep."

"Damn the cost!" Thomas Meagher exclaimed. "We

have the money, and what is it for but to help you become the greatest lawyer in all Ireland?"

"I can learn the law in other ways," Tom pointed out. "In Dublin I could study with a fine lawyer. Perhaps I will learn more and quicker in that way."

Thomas Meagher could not shake his son's resolve. Finally, he gave in. "On one condition," he told Tom. "To be a well-rounded man you need to know how people live. People other than the English and the Irish. Your twentieth birthday is but two months away. As a birthday gift, accept a trip to France, Germany, Holland and Belgium. It is but a small part of expenses at a university and will do much for your understanding of human needs. Accept it and I will say no more about further schooling."

Tom agreed. He spent the following six weeks traveling through western Europe. He expected much of his visit to France, but was sorely disappointed. The great French Revolution ending in 1792 had been followed by another uprising less than forty years later. Sandwiched in between had been the rise and fall of Napoleon. And now, with Louis Philippe as king, the lesser citizens of France expected relief.

Louis Philippe—called King of the Middle Classes and Citizen King—had known hard work and poverty, and he tried to make France prosperous.. He failed. His own people finally learned to hate and despise the man they had considered their savior. Finding the French people as steeped in misery as his own, Tom moved on to Germany.

During the previous century one German ruler after another had pledged himself to establish a constitution that gave the people a share of the government. Sparks of revolt had flashed now and then in various German states, but nothing of consequence had happened. Frederick William IV had just succeeded to the throne when Tom arrived. There was a kind of peace in the country, and a prosperity. But Frederick William, as had all the Hohenzollern rulers, firmly believed in the divine right of kings. It would be years before the people of Germany would have any say.

Tom found the situation considerably better in both Holland and Belgium. Each had been independent for ten years. Both had established constitutional monarchies and were in effect democracies.

Tom returned to Ireland hardly encouraged by what he had seen. It seemed to him that, even with the passing of centuries, subject peoples found it impossible to achieve their just rights. Yet, he thought, there were the American colonies. They had achieved their independence of England in a relatively short span of years.

A few days after his twentieth birthday Tom Meagher moved to Dublin, taking a position as apprentice law clerk in the capital's largest law office. He worked long hours, driving himself as if even a moment lost would retard his progress a lifetime.

The little freedom he allowed himself was spent in exploring the ancient city, the scene of so much of Ireland's tragedy as well as history. There was much to see, so much he had missed on his previous and brief visits.

He walked along the banks of the Liffey River, looked out over Dublin Bay, marveling at the beauty that was his Ireland.

Regal, impressive Dublin Castle, originally built early in the thirteenth century, fascinated him. The king's deputies had ruled Ireland from the old fortress. There, in its grim Kilmainham Gaol, a hulking horror of stone, the deputies had executed hundreds of Irish patriots, many of whose names were scratched eerily into the walls of the cells. C759140

His most thrilling moments were those spent exploring Trinity College, founded by Queen Elizabeth in 1591. A five-minute walk from his law office in the heart of Dublin, and set in the midst of thirty-seven acres of tree-shaded, lush green lawns, it was Tom's favorite lunch-hour retreat. He found an inner peace walking along its winding paths, examining its historic treasures.

In the wood-walled Long Room of Trinity's time-worn library the famous Book of Kells was displayed. Never, Tom believed, had he ever seen anything more inspiring and more beautiful than this illuminated manuscript of the Four Gospels, written perhaps ten centuries before.

"It's a shame," the guide explained, "that the beautiful golden cover was destroyed."

Not only a shame, Tom thought, but a tragedy that such an exquisite work of Celtic art should have been damaged in the least. He could visualize the holy monks at St. Columba's Monastery in County Meath, just west of Dublin, as they worked lovingly and painstakingly over a thousand years before. The artistry in the initial letters of the Gospel chapters was exquisitely delicate, almost microscopic in its tracings, and brightened with delightful Irish whimsies—men pulling each other's beards, birds and dragons, cats chasing mice.

But what of Jonathan Swift, the most famous graduate of Trinity College? Nowhere could Tom find any indication that the caustic, satirical creator of *Gulliver's Travels* had ever studied there. One would think that, after a hundred years, this more English than Irish native of Dublin would be honored by the Protestant school.

During the last week of August, that year of 1843, Daniel O'Connell was scheduled to speak at a large meeting sponsored by the Loyal National Repeal Association he had founded three years previously. Tom allowed nothing to keep him from attending that meeting at Tara Hill, the seat of Ireland's ancient kings, located in County Meath just northwest of Dublin.

Tom arrived at Tara early. Already thousands of people were scattered around the foot and along the sides of the hill. Carts and carriages dotted the grassy approaches, the horses unhitched and grazing nearby. It was five hundred feet up a gradual slope to the crest of the hill where the speaker's platform had been built. Tom was glad he came early.

He walked slowly to the top to be as near the great patriot as possible, so as not to miss a single word. Halfway up he turned to look down. Even at that distance faces around the base were blurred and he wondered how those who remained below might hear. He finally reached the top and seated himself on the grass near one of the many bands which ringed the platform, listening to the stirring music as first one and then another blared forth.

Tom had sat there, he did not know how long, looking out over the Irish countryside as he had so often from Mount Misery, when a great roar broke his reverie. He swung himself around to face the platform. In the center, surrounded by priests and bishops, was Daniel O'Connell, both hands raised high.

Tom had seen the man before, but never at such close range. He was a most impressive sight. Tall and sturdy as an oak, Tom thought, the picture of strength as he stood there, smiling and waving his hands. And not merely physical strength. Yet the lines around his clear blue eyes seemed mute testimony of how tired he must be.

The crowd hushed as a priest moved beside O'Connell to open the meeting with a prayer. Tom recognized him as one of the most famous in Ireland, Father Theobald Matthew, a Capuchin Franciscan, known to all Irishmen as the Apostle of Temperance. Father Matthew, a dedicated social worker who was deeply concerned about the plight of his people, had persuaded thousands of Irishmen to take the pledge of total abstinence.

As the priest finished the prayer and "Amen" echoed from all about Tara Hill, Daniel O'Connell moved forward. He began to speak. Tom felt himself stimulated with the first words, the voice was so resonant and rich, so authoritative. And, he smiled inwardly in satisfaction, there was more than a touch of Irish brogue.

O'Connell began his speech by recounting, in stirring tones, the many injustices perpetrated by England. He went on to bemoan the lack of compassion for the impoverished Irish.

"And what can we do to help ourselves?" he went on. "We have not the men nor the arms to stand up against the soldiers of England, the strongest nation in all the world. No! To battle them on their own terms would be the fool's way. But there is something we can do. If every Irishman, especially all Catholics, because they are in the great majority, will work with one another, all band together, we will, in time, achieve our freedom without bloodshed. If all of us, united, show ourselves as firm in our demands, peaceful in our protests, England will have to give Ireland justice and freedom. Protest, demonstrate, but do so peacefully and bear with me and I promise you Ireland will be free within six months!"

Tom returned to Dublin after the speech, confused. He realized that earlier attempts at armed rebellion had failed, but was Daniel O'Connell telling Ireland that it should sit back, do nothing but protest and wait for England to respond? And meanwhile more hundreds would die of poverty and disease, more thousands would leave their homelands for Australia, New Zealand and America. It seemed to Tom that action, immediate action, was needed. Verbal protests had been made again and again—and by O'Connell himself—yet what had they accomplished? True, some concessions had been made. But they were primarily paper concessions that left Ireland still in bondage. Was an appeal to England's conscience really Ireland's best chance?

Through the following weeks Thomas Meagher's mind returned again and again to the problem. Always there was one factor he could not overlook. Daniel O'Connell, surely, knew what he was saying. No single Irishman in years had done half so much good. No more loyal Irishman lived. Surely so wise a man had good reason for his course of action, however fruitless it might seem. Until he could think of a more practical course, he would have to keep faith with O'Connell. And the man had promised that Ireland would be free within six months.

Another great meeting, Tom learned, was planned for September 25 at Lismore, west of Waterford in southern Ireland. It was to be preceded by a dinner on the night of the twenty-fourth honoring O'Connell. Tom decided he would attend both the dinner and the meeting and casually mentioned it to his father on a visit to Waterford.

"There is your chance, Tom," his father told him. "You must be included as a speaker at the dinner for O'Connell."

Tom shook his head. "I have made no name for myself yet, Father," he said. "Besides, how can I walk in and say, Look here, I am Thomas Meagher and wish to speak? It will take influence for any man, so unknown, to be included as a speaker at so fine a gathering."

His father laughed. "Tom," he said, "you forget that

the mayor of Waterford is your father! Wouldn't that give you some influence?"

The evening of September 24, 1843, twenty-year-old Thomas Meagher made his first political speech, with Daniel O'Connell, recognized as one of the greatest orators in the world, looking on.

Thomas Meagher approached the podium that night quaking inside, but trying to maintain a show of self-confidence. Recognizing his youth and inexperience as contrasted with the sixty-eight-year-old O'Connell, he had decided to make his speech short, raise a question or two and then urge patience for the plan offered by the aging patriot.

"It has been said that peaceful protests do not bring us our freedom," he said, his voice strong and resonant. "Time has proved this. Perhaps we should look for other means to make ourselves felt and heard. The American colonies tried to reason with England. They did not succeed, and finally took up arms in a full rebellion. Perhaps we may come to that. Perhaps that will be our only successful course. But I say for now we must listen to the man who has accomplished so much for us. Daniel O'Connell has promised us freedom in six months. To those, young and impatient like myself, to those of us who decry the cold hearts of England, hearts we have not reached with cold logic, and ache to strike with cold steel, to all such of us I say let us be patient. With God's help Daniel O'Connell may yet bring peace and freedom, food and prosperity to Ireland."

A rising surge of applause escorted Thomas Meagher

back to his seat, though he did hear a few shouts of protest from young voices throughout the hall. When Tom had taken his seat, the chairman of the meeting rose and introduced Daniel O'Connell. But Ireland's greatest champion did not go immediately to the podium.

Smiling broadly, O'Connell first walked to where Tom was seated. He forced him to rise to another, and more tumultuous, round of applause, and clapped him warmly on the shoulders.

"Well done," Daniel O'Connell said to Tom, speaking loudly enough so that his words could be heard throughout the room. "Well done, Young Ireland!"

IV
THE BLACK SHADOWS
LENGTHEN

His first political speech, and the tremendous compliment paid him by Daniel O'Connell, pushed young Thomas Meagher prematurely into the Irish limelight. He had decided the day after the dinner, as he listened to O'Connell at Lismore, that he was not ready for total involvement. He had too much to learn and his work in the law office had become too time consuming. Besides, though he was more and more in disagreement with O'Connell's "peace plan" to force England's hand, he still felt the man should be given a chance.

Tom now could not walk down a Dublin street without being hailed by strangers, even stopped for his opinions. And he was continually being invited to speak at this meeting or that. He accepted none of the invitations.

O'Connell himself, perhaps conscious of the rising sentiment against peaceful resistance, and perhaps equally conscious of the too quick passing of the six-month period, increased the frequency of the rallies at which he spoke. The meetings drew larger and larger crowds. They became more unruly and more difficult to control.

Tom attended many of these meetings. He marveled at the way O'Connell was able to quiet every disturbance before it erupted into open disorder. He realized, as O'Connell must have, that England hoped that rioting and lawlessness would result from one of the meetings. English soldiers would then have an excuse to move in, arrest O'Connell and still his voice. It never came about. O'Connell—dubbed by his followers the Uncrowned King of Ireland—was too persuasive and too popular. He always silenced the growing crowds in time.

The English could not wait. They were afraid it was only a matter of days before the seething unrest would explode. It would be dangerous, the English deputies decided, to wait for a legitimate excuse for O'Connell's arrest.

A fight broke out between two men at a meeting during O'Connell's speech. Was the antagonist a plant by the English? No one knew, and the English soldiers obviously didn't care. Ignoring the two battlers, a contingent of armed soldiers moved to the platform and arrested Daniel O'Connell "in the name of the Queen" for inciting and inflaming the populace to riot. He was rushed off to Newgate Prison.

Thomas Meagher had not attended that particular meeting. Hearing of it, he fumed at the patently trumped-up charges on which O'Connell was held. He made a point of attending each session of the trial held at the Queen's Bench in Dublin. He barely controlled himself, overcome with anger and disgust at the total unfairness of the proceedings. But there was nothing he could do. The trial was a preplanned farce.

The presiding judge was English. He allowed the defense no advantage, however small. He permitted the selection of an all-English jury. No testimony relating to O'Connell's long-recognized pleading for peaceful protest was admitted in evidence. As everyone expected, Daniel O'Connell was quickly adjudged guilty as charged. He was fined and sentenced to a year in prison.

During the few months just past, a hundred or more young Irishmen, mostly recent college graduates, had joined O'Connell's Catholic Association dedicated to repeal of the detested Act of Union which bound Ireland to England. Embittered by the gross injustice to O'Connell, Tom Meagher waited no longer. He also joined the Repeal Movement, determined to help continue O'Connell's work while the patriot was in prison.

O'Connell was released after he had served three months. He came out of jail lacking much of his earlier fire, his spirit broken. The many weeks in prison had sapped him physically. The collapse of his dream of bringing freedom to Ireland within six months had left him heartbroken. Nonetheless, he stubbornly insisted that only his "peaceful" resistance would help Ireland.

The influx of impatient young men into the association was bound to mean trouble within the Repeal Movement. It came all too soon, for as the summer of 1845 came to a close Ireland was near total collapse. The potato crop had all but disappeared. Famine swept the island.

By that time over a half million people had died of starvation and disease. More than a million more had left Ireland for other lands, the majority migrating to the United States. The English government was aware of the dire straits of the Irish. In Parliament the subject was continually debated, but little was done. America, and many European countries, sent boatloads of food to help ease Irish hunger, but distribution procedures were woefully inadequate, and precious little reached Ireland's starving population.

Business meetings of the Repeal Movement evolved into unending debates. The young shouted for a change in policy, for out-and-out attack on the English. Adherents of O'Connell's plan were just as loud in their support of patience. A meeting of minds seemed impossible.

The youth contingent in the Repeal Movement made the first break. They met in secret to develop a course of action. Thomas Meagher was chairman of the meeting.

"We cannot continue in this way," a young man named Terence McCormick told the assembly. "The English do nothing but hit us again and again. We only turn the other cheek. We will get nowhere fighting with words."

"Do you have a suggestion, Mr. McCormick?" Meagher asked from the platform.

"Perhaps. Why can't we break away from the association of O'Connell and fight our own battles as we agree among ourselves?"

A great cheer went up. Not a single voice was raised in protest against leaving the established group.

"It seems you are not alone in your thinking, Terence,"

Thomas Meagher said. "So be it. But what shall we call our splinter?"

There were some moments of debate as one suggestion after another was made. Then Michael Riordan spoke up.

"I was at Lismore when you spoke for the first time, Tom," he said, "and I well recall O'Connell's saying, 'Well done, Young Ireland.' Let us call ourselves Young Ireland, for that is what we are!"

The name was adopted without further debate.

"Well!" Tom Meagher announced from the platform. "We are now Young Ireland. We know that the Repealers' philosophy calls for gaining Ireland's freedom by working peacefully with the English. We do not wish to be labeled as hotheads with no regard for bloodshed."

Michael Riordan again jumped to his feet. "On that I agree!" he called out. "But we think differently from them. And we must have a distinction. It is my thought that we work hand-in-glove with the Repealers for our common aim. Yet it must be our determination to take up arms if necessary in fighting for our liberties."

The hall rocked with shouts and applause. Thomas Meagher was elected leader of Young Ireland, and Michael Riordan his first lieutenant. Another decision made that night was to publish a newspaper, to be called *The Nation.*

"We need such a paper," Meagher announced, "so that the Irish people will know and understand our principles, to know and understand the wrongs being done them and how they can help to right those wrongs."

During the months ahead Young Ireland grew in strength. Though there was no great difference as yet in the open activities of Young Ireland as compared with O'Connell's Repealers, they made a significant impression throughout the island. In October 1846 over three thousand came to Dublin's Rotunda Hall to hear Thomas Meagher speak.

Daniel O'Connell revealed his true greatness when he learned of the tremendous success of the Young Ireland group. "They must rejoin us," he told one of his friends. "They can be a great power for good and young Thomas Meagher is an excellent leader and speaker. I am writing him and asking that he return to the Repeal Association."

Tom Meagher's eyes filled with tears as he read O'Connell's letter. He had great respect for the aged patriot, but his first obligation was to Ireland. Back in the association he and his Young Ireland group would be hamstrung. And the time was nearing for action on their part.

Tom answered O'Connell's letter, expressing deep regret at being unable to recommend a rejoining of the Young Irelands with the Repeal Movement. In conscience he could not do so, he wrote, because he did not believe anything could be achieved by the wait-and-see methods of the association.

As the year 1847 dawned, famine was still rampant in Ireland, as was disease. Deaths were increasing. There was need for action. The situation was analyzed and discussed at a meeting of Young Ireland in Dublin. While Young Ireland's publication, *The Nation,* had been most effective in spreading the story of Ireland's plight among Irish citizens, it was felt that Young Ireland had outlived its usefulness.

"We are looked upon too much as another Repeal Movement, since we have patiently followed the non-violence philosophy of Daniel O'Connell," young Michael Riordan told the meeting. "We must give ourselves a new and more militant image. We must be known for action."

"Perhaps we should reorganize," Thomas Meagher suggested.

"We need do more than merely that," exclaimed another firebrand named Dennis Riley. "Why not begin making trouble for the English?"

"Trouble for trouble's sake will only shed our blood," Thomas pointed out. "Remember we are outnumbered greatly. No, we must move carefully, though I agree we must move in some manner. We need more men, a stronger organization."

"Thomas," Michael Riordan said, "why not establish chapters throughout Ireland?"

So it was decided. Young Ireland was dissolved and in its place Meagher and his friends founded a new organization they called the Irish Confederation. Before the year had passed, the confederation had grown to a membership nearing thirteen thousand young men, with confederation chapters located throughout Ireland.

The satisfaction Tom felt at such success disappeared when the news came that Daniel O'Connell was dead. He had respected the old man for all he had tried to do, loved him for his dedication to Ireland. It was a crushing blow. Even though he disagreed with many of O'Connell's methods, Tom felt deeply that Ireland could ill afford the loss.

A month after the confederation was established, Tom's father visited him in Dublin. The elder Thomas Meagher had been elected to Parliament as a representative from Waterford and was on his way to London.

"This idea of a confederation is excellent, Tom," he told his son. "But I think it is not enough. Why not enter your name as a candidate for Parliament?"

"But, Father," Tom said, "Daniel O'Connell, Junior, is now the representative from Waterford. It would be bad to run against him. I could not."

"Young O'Connell is resigning his seat," Thomas Meagher pointed out. "I heard it from his own lips before I left home."

Tom was uncertain. "I don't know," he said. "A campaign is costly."

Thomas Meagher shook his head. "Not so costly it would not be worth the good it might do," he said. "And don't worry about the money. I will see that you have enough to carry on a good fight."

Tom entered the race the moment the younger Daniel O'Connell's resignation was announced. The campaign was a bitter one. His opponent, backed by English partisans, derided his youth and lack of experience in an attempt to counteract Tom's growing popularity. The election was close. In the end Thomas Meagher was defeated by just a few votes.

Tom, though embarrassed by the defeat, was not disappointed. He had felt all along that he could do more good outside Parliament, furthering the work of the confederation. He became more certain as news of one revolution after the other began filtering through from the European mainland early in 1848.

In France the citizens, tired of promises and demanding electoral reform, deposed King Louis Philippe and took over the government. Philippe fled to England. In Germany an attempt was made to overthrow the government. There was unrest in Italy, Poland and Russia. Revolution was so much the order of the day in 1848 that it was called the Revolutionary Year.

The rebellion in France, and the unsettled conditions promising revolt in the other European countries, made Thomas Meagher feel certain that it was time for an all-out effort in Ireland. Nor was he alone in his thinking. As news of the French uprising swept across Ireland, a new newspaper began circulation in the island.

John Mitchel, one of the original Young Ireland group who had written for *The Nation,* began publishing *The United Irishman.* Mitchel, far more militant than any of the young Irishmen, openly advocated armed revolt against England. His paper proclaimed, "Our independence must be won at all hazards."

By midsummer, roiled by Mitchel's editorials, Ireland was ready to explode. To ease the tension, O'Connell's Repeal Movement scheduled a July meeting in Dublin. John O'Connell, younger son of Daniel, was chairman of the meeting. It was decided that the affair should be given broad appeal and present varying views. So young Thomas Meagher, recognized by now, with the elder O'Connell dead, as Ireland's finest orator, should be included as a speaker.

Tom, certain that the time for action was long past, spoke clearly and with authority. "Surely, the facts are clear," he told the large audience. "The soldier is proof against an argument. He is not proof against a bullet. The man that will listen to reason, let him be reasoned with. But it is the weaponed arm of the patriot that alone can prevail against battalioned despotism."

There was a stir in the crowd. It was not the sort of talk they expected from the Repeal Movement. But, of course, Thomas Meagher had long before disassociated himself from that group.

"I do not condemn the use of arms as immoral," Tom continued. "Nor do I conceive it to be profane to say that the King of Heaven bestows his benediction upon those who unsheath the sword in the hour of a nation's peril."

Tom became conscious of activity behind on the platform. From the corner of his eye he could see young John O'Connell, face crimson, inwardly fuming. He was not deterred.

"Abhor the sword?" he went on. "No! For in the passes of the Tyrol, it cut to pieces the banner of the Bavarian. Abhor the sword? No! For at its blow a great nation started from the waters of the Atlantic, and the crippled colony sprang into the attitude of a proud republic—prosperous, limitless and invincible."

The crowd had been stirred as never before. Meagher's words, delivered with strength and in ringing tones, had almost everyone in the huge hall on his feet, shouting and cheering. From the platform came the insistent rap of the gavel. It did not quiet the crowd.

"Stop!" John O'Connell shouted, his words drowned out by the cheers. Tom, however, could hear the chairman clearly.

"This is not the way of the Repeal Movement!" O'Connell was screaming. "We cannot permit you to continue, Meagher!"

The crowd quieted slightly, waiting for Tom to go on. Now they heard the chairman's wild ranting.

"Everything you say is against the peaceful principles advanced by my father! We will have no part of it!"

Bedlam erupted in the great hall. Some cheered Meagher on, calling out, "Well said, Tom!" "God bless the sword!" "God bless Thomas Meagher!" Others, trying to drown them out, shouted to the ceiling: "Get your own hall!" "Get out!"

A few fights broke out. The meeting was near total disruption. Tom, conscious of the possible aftermath of continued arguments and fights which might bring on the English soldiers, tried to calm his partisans. He succeeded only when he left the platform and started for the door with hundreds of his sympathizers following.

The die had been cast. The differences between the Repeal Movement and the Irish Confederation were now sharply defined. Where only *The United Irishmen* of John Mitchel had been openly supporting revolt as the answer to Ireland's problems, now *The Nation,* published by the Meagher group, followed suit.

All Ireland was soon ablaze with revolutionary fire. From Malin Head at the far north to Mizen Head in the south, over the span of near three hundred miles that separates the capes, Irish hills echoed the resolve to bear arms, if need be, to achieve freedom. Another symbol of Irish rebellion made its appearance. The Meagher group unfurled a new flag, inspired by the French revolutionaries, who had replaced the fleurs-de-lis with a tricolor. The Irish now had their green, white and gold tricolor. Action would no longer take place under cover. Everything would be done openly, and the devil take the English!

England itself was also seething. The London clerk, the Liverpool dock worker, the peasant—all were grumbling. Suffering injustices themselves, the downtrodden English were openly sympathizing with the suffering Irish. All over England the demand for relief was heard, relief not only for the underprivileged English but also for their counterparts across the Irish Sea. Revolution seemed imminent even in Great Britain itself. The situation was so explosive that Queen Victoria and the royal family were whisked away from London for asylum on the Isle of Wight.

The English deputies, charged with maintaining order, decided to make an example of the most violent of the Irish rebels. They arrested John Mitchel and remanded him to prison without bail, pending trial on a charge of sedition.

Mitchel was undaunted. He reveled in his arrest, calling out from his cell to the crowds outside the prison, "They have indicted me for sedition, but I tell them that I intend to commit high treason!"

Fully aware that he might soon share a cell with Mitchel, Thomas Meagher charged ahead. He felt sure the time for forcing England's hand had come. His speeches became more and more inflammatory. At a public meeting in Dublin he exclaimed, "The time has come for every Irishman to speak out. I declare myself the enemy of the government. Let the demand for the reconstruction of the nationality of Ireland be constitutionally made. If nothing comes of this, then up with the barricades and invoke the God of Battles!"

The deputies had anticipated Meagher. They had sent agents to the meeting to take down his speech. William Smith O'Brien, chairman of the meeting, and Thomas Meagher, its principal speaker, were both arrested on a charge of sedition. Both, however, were granted bail and released immediately.

Like Mitchel, Meagher was not cowed by his arrest. As he left the police barracks, he stopped to address the crowd milling outside. "I shall speak to the judge," he told them, "the jury and the prosecuting underlings of this thuglike government. I shall tell them to their faces that I have spoken sedition, and that I glory in it. One circumstance alone shall stop me—my death!" The crowd cheered and carried Thomas Meagher down the street.

Thomas Meagher's trial was held on March 16. The prosecution paraded witness after witness testifying to

Tom's open defiance of England. The agents read their transcript of his speech. Somehow, the prosecution had made mistakes in the seating of the jury. The panel failed to agree on a verdict, and Tom, along with William Smith O'Brien, walked free from the courtroom.

"There is no doubt in my mind that they will have me back," he told the hundreds cheering him outside Queen's Bench. "But let them; I am ready for whatever they do!"

That night there was a great celebration honoring the release of Thomas Meagher and William Smith O'Brien. Thousands came from all around Dublin to parade through the streets. A wild, noisy demonstration made its way to the prison, shouting and screaming for the release of John Mitchel.

England's hand was forced prematurely. The deputies had hoped to quiet Mitchel by keeping him in jail. But an imprisoned John Mitchel was proving as much a danger as a free one. The March 18 edition of *The United Irishmen* carried a story by him. "We await attack," he wrote. "We shall not provoke the shedding of blood; but if blood be shed, we shall see the end of it."

Mitchel was quickly brought to trial. The prosecution, hurried in its case, again failed to impanel a jury fully committed to the English. Again the jury failed to agree and John Mitchel was released.

A few days later Thomas Meagher and John Mitchel met to discuss strategy. Both realized that their luck would not last. England would find some way to jail them for good. An all-out maneuver by the Irish was vital.

"Tom," Mitchel said, "we must take advantage of the

success of others. France accomplished what we hope to do. Perhaps it will help us to know how they drove out Louis Philippe."

Tom nodded. "I've just heard that Milan has again freed itself of Austrian control. The citizens there forced the Austrian garrison out of the city. We should be able to drive out the English soldiers."

"God willing!" Mitchel said. "But it will take planning. Why cannot you and a small group go to Paris and learn, on the spot, whether any of their plans would help us?"

"Wouldn't it be better if you went, or at least came along?" Tom asked.

Mitchel shook his head. "The English watch me too closely," he said. "And one of us should remain here to keep the pot boiling. I have in mind a giant mass meeting while you are gone to divert the deputies, and also to serve as a warning to them that we have reached the end of our patience."

The following day, accompanied by William Smith O'Brien, Michael Riordan and Terence McCormick, Thomas Meagher left for Paris. As they boarded a carriage in Dublin, Confederation Clubs from all around central Ireland were massing in downtown Dublin. Nearly fifteen thousand had answered Mitchel's call. Organized into battle formation, but unarmed, they marched in military precision to Dublin's music hall, passing between cheering thousands, with other thousands milling about the entrance to the hall.

John Mitchel gave a typical, rousing speech. As he con-

cluded, an Irishman approached the platform carrying
a long wooden shaft with a pointed steel head.

"Mr. Mitchel," the man said, handing the shaft to
John, "I give you this pike, which has long been the
traditional weapon of the Irish peasant."

Mitchel held the pike high over his head. "Look at it!"
he called out to the crowd. "This is still a most usable
weapon. I tell you now that within a week you will see
pikes openly displayed all over Dublin!"

By the time Thomas Meagher returned from Paris,
stores in Dublin were openly selling pikes. The government was helpless to control the sale. The existing laws,
as proved by the releases of Meagher, Mitchel and
O'Brien, were not strong enough. Prodded by the Dublin
deputies, Parliament moved quickly. They passed the
Treason and Felony Act, providing that certain specified
seditious or disloyal acts by any citizen would be punished
by exile, called transportation for life. Those found
guilty under the act would be sent to such sparsely populated British possessions, far removed from the British
Isles, as New Zealand, Tasmania and Australia.

The Treason and Felony Act also tightened court procedures. No more could a prisoner, before trial, be released on bail. In this way, Parliament rationalized, the
prisoner would be hamstrung in trying to prepare a defense. Guilty verdicts would be more easily obtained
from juries. Parliament did not hesitate to make it known
that the Treason and Felony Act had been specially prepared to straitjacket men like Mitchel and Meagher.

To give the new law even stronger teeth, the Lord

Lieutenant of Ireland, Lord Clarendon, decreed that all unauthorized parades and demonstrations would be considered treason. He issued a proclamation to that effect and had thousands of notices placed throughout Dublin.

Thomas Meagher and Michael Riordan saw the first of these notices as they walked near Dublin Castle. "Look at that!" Thomas said, pointing. "His excellency now forbids the Irish to assemble, even peaceably, unless he gives us his blessing!"

Riordan contemplated the poster for a moment. "Surely," he said, "what the Lord Lieutenant has done, we can do. I have an idea. I will put up a few posters myself!"

In the dead of night, with the help of a dozen or so young men, Michael Riordan posted a second notice beside that of the Lord Lieutenant. It reminded the Irish of Dublin of their rights and dared the English to interfere in any way.

Though the Treason and Felony Act had been aimed at them, Thomas Meagher and John Mitchel laughed it off. Neither had feared jail before. Both were convinced that the government would be overthrown long before either could be tried and sent away to the south Pacific.

Tom's disdain for the new law was immediately evident. His trip to France had taught him that arms were necessary. He began arming the Grattans, his Confederation Club, with rifles and pikes. He laid out his own money for the arms of every member unable to afford the equipment himself. Other clubs, whose members were less affluent, armed their people with eight-foot pikes.

Thomas Meagher and his lieutenants began touring the various organized and armed clubs in Ireland to begin training the members. They were assisted by young Irishmen who had served in the British army, many of whom deserted in order to join the Irish cause. Recruits were drilled and trained throughout Ireland in deserted farmyards and city cellars.

No secret had been made of the arming of Irish citizens. The Lord Lieutenant called a secret meeting to plan a disarming of the Irish. Soldiers would station themselves at cross streets to keep individuals from entering or leaving a district. While the blockade was in effect, other soldiers would search the houses, confiscating the arms and arresting the inhabitants. This plan did not get off the ground. Its details were leaked to the Irish rebels and the soldiers found nothing.

The various Confederation Clubs proceeded with their training. It was only a matter of weeks before they would be ready to make a concerted drive to overthrow the English government in Ireland. Lord Clarendon became increasingly alarmed. He ordered the arrest of John Mitchel for treason. Mitchel was jailed at Newgate Prison without bail, under the terms of the Treason and Felony Act.

There was no doubt in the minds of the Irish that the government would make certain that the jury would be composed only of men sympathetic to their own cause. To formulate plans to assure Mitchel's receiving a fair trial, a giant open-air meeting was announced for the Sunday following his arrest. Some confederation mem-

bers vowed the meeting would also be forced to consider
ways to rescue Mitchel. "We must do so," they proclaimed openly, "if we have to tear the goal apart stone
by stone."

Lord Clarendon settled on a plan to end the meeting
before it got under way. He ordered the city police of
Dublin to form cordons across all streets approaching
the meeting site. That Sunday, as the Irish marched toward the open park where the meeting was to be held,
over four hundred policemen stood side-to-side blockad-
ing the roads. But the Lord Lieutenant had made a bad
choice. As the marching men neared, the police swung
around to form a guard between which the marchers
proceeded unharmed. The meeting began and ended
without incident.

The agitation for forcible release of John Mitchel disturbed Thomas Meagher. He had analyzed the situation,
hoping that there might be sufficient strength among
their forces to affect a rescue. He finally decided it was a
foolhardy plan which not only had no chance of success,
but would result in Irish blood being spilled.

John Mitchel was tried. As everyone expected, he was
found guilty.

"John Mitchel," the presiding judge intoned after the
verdict was read, "you have been found guilty of treason
to Her Majesty the Queen. Have you anything to say
in your behalf before sentence is passed upon you?"

Mitchel faced the judge squarely. "I have been tried
by a packed jury," he said evenly. "By the jury of a par-

tisan sheriff. By a packed jury obtained by a juggle. I object to any sentence being passed upon me."

The judge ignored Mitchel's words. He pronounced sentence: transportation for fourteen years.

Mitchel had more to say. "Neither the jury nor the judges nor any other man in this court presumes to imagine that it is a criminal who stands in this dock," he told the court. "The Roman who saw his hand burning to ashes promised the tyrant that three hundred should follow to carry on for him. Can I not promise for one or two or three or—aye!—for hundreds of hundreds?" He turned and pointed around the courtroom at Irish patriots including Thomas Meagher, Terence McCormick, Sean Hickey and Michael Riordan.

Immediately, and almost in a single voice, the courtroom echoed with cries of "And I!" "Add my name, John Mitchel!" "I'm with you, John!"

The massed Irish in the courtroom seemed ready to charge the dock. The sheriff moved forward quickly. With the help of deputies he grabbed John Mitchel's arm and rushed him out through a side door. Taking but a moment to clamp irons on the man's wrists and ankles, they whisked John Mitchel away to the Dublin pier, where the ship *Sheerwater* was ready to sail for Australia.

The loss of John Mitchel placed a greater burden on Thomas Meagher's shoulders. It also relieved him of the need to keep the fires of enthusiasm burning in the Irish hearts. The manner in which Mitchel had been railroaded stirred Ireland to fever pitch. Membership in the

Confederation Clubs doubled within six months. There was no doubt now that unity was the great Irish hope. There had to be organization, coordinated planning and complete arming of the masses.

Tom realized, too, that total and thorough preparation was necessary before an open fight could be risked. In a secret meeting a decision was made. The password "harvest time" became the undercover designation for the planned uprising against the government. Until then, Tom, and every Irish leader, would be busy checking arms and supplies, and the progress of training throughout Ireland.

On July 11, having completed a tour of inspection of Confederation Clubs in Cork, Limerick and Tipperary counties of Munster Province, Tom stopped at his home in Waterford. His father had returned from London for a holiday.

They had just finished supper when a knock was heard. The elder Thomas Meagher went to the door. Outside stood a captain of the English army and a constable.

"I am looking for Thomas Francis Meagher," the captain told Tom's father.

Hearing his name, Tom came to the door. "I am Thomas Francis Meagher," he said, knowing what would come.

"I have a warrant for your arrest," the captain said.

"On what charge?"

"Using seditious language," was the answer.

Tom was surprised. It was a mild charge compared to

that on which Mitchel had been arrested. And it was a bailable charge.

Taken to Dublin, Thomas Meagher was arraigned on the charge, then released under heavy bail. Trial date was set for September, during the next Limerick assizes.

V

"TO BE HANGED
BY THE NECK..."

Thomas Meagher was undaunted by either his arrest or his impending trial. A meeting had already been scheduled for July 16, only five days after the arrest. It was to be an outdoor affair, on Slievenamon Hill. Located in Munster Province, near a point where the Counties of Tipperary, Kilkenny and Waterford meet, Slievenamon rose more than twenty-three hundred feet. It had been the site of many resistances during Ireland's turbulent history. Tom and Sean Hickey had selected the location for its significance.

"We should cancel the meeting," Sean told Tom the morning after his release on bail. "It would be a great danger to your case to go on with our plan."

Tom thought for a moment, then shook his head. "We must go on, Sean," he said. "More harm could come to the cause than to me, if we do not hold the meeting. The people's enthusiasm and spirit for fighting the enemy must be kept high. If they see one of us showing the white feather—we can't chance it."

"But the barracks at Carrick-on-Suir is bound to be reinforced with extra soldiers and police, all armed," Sean protested.

"All the better," Tom replied. "Let them realize we do not fear them. Let them know we recognize our God-given rights and will dare death to get them."

July 16 dawned bright and hot. Despite the heat of the day and the long, tiring climb to the crest of Slievenamon, the roads leading to the Femham Plain at the base of the mountain were choked with patriots. From Tralee and Cloghane in the west they came, and from Wexford, Kilcoole and Dublin on the Irish Sea to the east. Roads from the south teemed with citizens of Youghal, Skibbereen and points between. Limerick, Roscommon and Sligo were well represented from the north.

When Thomas Meagher as principal speaker came to the center of the platform, he could see hardly any patch of green on the verdant slopes of Slievenamon, so great was the crowd. More than sixty thousand Irishmen had sent up a roar as he came forward, his shock of red hair covered by a green, round-topped hat with a gold band, and a bright three-colored sash—green, white and gold, the colors of the new flag—angled from shoulder to waist. "What there is to report," he told the teeming thousands, "has already been spoken by the loyal sons of the green who came before me. But I stand here to dare the government to do worse than merely arrest me. What I have said and done has been said and done because I lived in a land of slavery. I feel that, if God gave me intellect, I must employ it for the good of my country. I have but one ambition and that is to decorate these hills and these lakes with Ireland's flag of freedom."

Wild cheers and shouts, lasting five minutes, interrupted Meagher. Sean Hickey turned to Michael Riordan beside him on the platform. "Such a roar I have never heard," he said. "Perhaps good Queen Vicky will have heard it herself in her sanctuary on the Isle of Wight."

Finally the tumult subsided and Thomas Meagher continued. "A scourge came from God," he said. "The pratie was smitten, yet your fields waved with golden corn and wheat. To your lips, however, both were forbidden fruit. English ships came and took it all away so that you and your neighbors and your friends starved. The evidence is plain to see. This land, which is yours as God's gift, is not yours by the law of England. Bayonets and guns have been placed between us and our rightful food."

The military barracks at Carrick-on-Suir was hardly five miles from Slievenamon Hill. Though the officers there were certainly aware of the illegal mass gathering, they did not move in. A detailed report of the open rebellion was, however, sent to Lord Clarendon. This latest slap at authority, he decided, had to be dealt with.

The first order was to disarm and disperse the Confederation Clubs. The second was to quarantine towns, cities and entire districts, especially those where confederation activity was strongest. Residents in quarantined areas were to surrender all arms and ammunition within four days or suffer a year's imprisonment. Clarendon issued a proclamation outlining his orders and had it posted in all public places in villages and cities under quarantine.

In Dublin, Thomas Meagher and Michael Riordan— as they had when a previous proclamation was posted— read the new posting together.

Riordan laughed. "His excellency did not learn from his earlier posting."

"Look, Michael," Thomas said, pointing at the poster. "Something new has been added by the good Lord Lieutenant: the English coat of arms."

"There's no hiding his authority now," Riordan put in. "I think you have a thought of countering Lord Clarendon's message."

"Right, indeed, Michael Riordan!" Thomas said, clapping Riordan on the back. "Two, as well as one, may play at this game of proclamations. Print some proclamations for us, as you once did. Make it strong and tell our confederation members they must disregard the Lord Lieutenant's order, keep their arms and hold together and wait for instructions."

"Should we not match the Lord Lieutenant and use an emblem as well?" Riordan asked.

"A capital idea!" Thomas exclaimed. "Where the royal coat of arms appears, use instead the gold harp of Tara on a green background. That was the emblem of those who fought for freedom before us."

The following morning the Lord Lieutenant's proclamation was accompanied by Meagher's posting in all

quarantined sections of Ireland. The placing of his message beside Lord Clarendon's orders was a wise decision.
The quarantine order had dashed the hopes of the Irish
loyals. Now their spirits were given a lift. Then, as the
Irish publications began printing pleas by the leaders
that no Irishman surrender his guns or other weaponry,
enthusiasm was restored to fever pitch.

On July 22 the chairmen of all the Confederation
Clubs met in Dublin and selected a five-man council. The
council, headed by Thomas Meagher, was to coordinate
all activities connected with the revolt and maintain supervision over all plans. Its first act was to send delegates
throughout Ireland to estimate the number of men who
might be depended upon for an all-out uprising in the
island, and the total of guns, weapons and ammunition
available in each district.

"We must also get outside help," Tom reported to the
meeting of the council. "Countries which have succeeded
in gaining liberty for the masses will no doubt be happy
to give Ireland support. France, perhaps, will send us an
army and also, we hope, its navy to close Irish ports to
English ships."

"How can we get this help?" asked John Devlin, a
council member.

"We must ask for it," Tom replied. "You know France,
John. Can you not get to Paris secretly and ask the
French government for help in the name of the council?"

John Devlin agreed. Other Irish patriots were assigned
similar missions to Holland, Belgium and Germany.

"You must do your work with speed," Meagher told

the emissaries. "We must make our big move quickly, otherwise we may find that time strengthens the English position."

The council debated for an hour before a decision was made. Finally, sometime between July 24 and 26 was agreed upon as the target date. The basic plan called for as near simultaneous attack on British garrisons throughout Ireland as communications at the time would permit.

By July 23 no word had been received from Devlin or the other agents. The council was called back into session.

"We can wait no longer," Thomas Meagher said. "If it is agreeable to all, let us set early morning of the twenty-sixth for the Rising. Our men know it as the final date agreed upon earlier. If help is to come, it should be here by that time."

The council settled down to discuss specific actions. The first decision was that Meagher and a handful of leaders would begin the revolt at some point in southern Ireland. Wexford, on St. George's Channel leading into the Irish Sea, was first suggested.

"I do not believe that is a good choice," one council member said. "Confederation Clubs had much difficulty there. We have not enough loyals at Wexford. It seems to me our first fire should be lighted where our forces are already well organized and prepared."

"I agree," another member put in. "Wexford is on the sea. The British might quickly shell the town by moving in the navy."

"A good point," Meagher agreed. "The same might apply to Waterford. But there is the village of Kilkenny. Though it is on the Nore River, the British would find it difficult to move gunboats through Waterford Harbour and up the Nore anywhere close to Kilkenny."

"Kilkenny is ideal," a council member stated. "We have perhaps five thousand armed men in the town itself."

"And its streets are narrow," another said. "They can be quickly and easily barricaded." He hesitated, then went on: "But what of the English military barracks at Kilkenny?"

"They are on the other side of the river from the town," Meagher said. "A few men might easily defend the bridge. If need be, the bridge could be destroyed."

Kilkenny was chosen unanimously as the location of the first assault on the enemy. Meagher, Michael Riordan and two others would go to Kilkenny and spark the first attack.

"Surprise must be our secret partner," Meagher announced finally. "We must catch the British unawares. So I propose that Terence McCormick be sent to Belfast to wait for word that the Rising has begun."

"For what purpose, Tom?" one member asked.

"My thought is that the moment I get word to Terence in Belfast that we have started our attack in Kilkenny, he will stir the Irish loyals there. If he remains under cover until that time, the British will be surprised. The military barracks in Belfast should be taken without difficulty then. And once that is done, a quick boarding of the few English ships might be accomplished."

"Are there enough armed men around Belfast to do so much?"

"Surely. But there is more. The ships taken over should then sail, with a thousand or more of our people aboard each, north past Larne and around Malin Head to the west coast and Killala Bay west of Sligo. From there they will take to land, add more armed men as they march south and meet with us coming up north. By that time we should have reached Athlone on Lough Ree."

It was an ingenious plan, perhaps too complex. One thing was certain: too much depended on effective communication, on immediate action once word was received. Meagher's instructions to the chairmen of the various Confederation Clubs were clear: They were to keep their members in readiness, prepared to attack the moment they heard Meagher's men had struck.

The biggest problem was Dublin. The strongest English detachment was located there. The rebels' great hope was that, once the blow was struck in Kilkenny, the English would rush soldiers south from Dublin to quell what they might consider a single uprising. With the defense weakened, Dublin would fall quickly. But there was to be activity of no kind in Dublin; nothing must be done that would alert the British, until Meagher had sent instructions. His orders would go to the chairman of the Dublin clubs and no one else. The chairman, and only the chairman, would order the attack in the capital.

Meagher sent his messenger to Dublin. The chairman was nowhere to be found. As a result not one shot was fired in the capital. Meagher had initiated the assault at

Kilkenny with only confusion as the result. He himself described the revolt as it broke open in Kilkenny:

"A torrent of human beings, rushing through lanes and narrow streets. Surging and boiling against the white basements that hemmed it in; with sounds of wrath, vengeance and defiance; clenched hands, waving to and fro, with wildest confusion in the air; eyes red with rage and desperation; long tresses of hair streaming in the roaring wind of voices; wild, half-stifled, passionate, frantic prayers of hope; invocation in sobs; challenges to the foe; curses on the red flag of England; scornful, exulting defiance of death; all wild as the winter gusts at sea, yet as black and fearful, too; this is what I beheld—these sounds I heard—such the dream that passed before me. It was the REVOLUTION, if we had accepted it. Why it was not accepted, I fear, I cannot with sufficient accuracy explain."

The confusion was complete. The collapse was total. Meagher kept a step ahead of the British soldiers, moving north. Some leaders were quickly captured and arrested. Others decamped and escaped, evading British patrols and making ther way to the Irish Sea or the Atlantic and boarding ships to freedom on the European mainland or in the United States.

On August 12 Thomas Meagher was finally cornered in central Ireland and arrested on a charge of high treason. He was taken to Dublin's Kilmainham Prison to await trial. A guilty verdict would mean death. Tom fully expected the worst. With the British in complete control of Ireland now that the rebellion had been smashed, there was no doubt that a pro-English jury would be impaneled to try him.

On Monday, October 16, in Clonmel, not far from his home town of Waterford, Thomas Francis Meagher was brought to trial. The formal charge was high treason against the government of Her Majesty, Victoria, Queen of England, Scotland and Ireland. There were two particulars in the charge: that Thomas Francis Meagher had waged war against Queen Victoria, that the same Thomas Francis Meagher had plotted the death of Her Majesty the Queen.

Ordered to rise in the prisoner's dock, Meagher was asked by the presiding judge: "Are you guilty or not guilty of the charges?"

"Not guilty," Meagher replied.

As he expected, the government took every precaution to seat a jury packed with English sympathizers. In four days the trial ended. On the fifth day the jury returned verdicts of guilty on both counts. On the seventh day the judge, ready to pass sentence, asked if he had anything to say.

"My lords," Meagher said, facing the bank of judges, "I wish to say a few words only. With my country I leave my memory, my sentiments, my acts, feeling proudly that they need no vindication from me. A jury has found me guilty. Influenced by the charge of the Lord Chief Justice, they could have found no other verdict. What of the charge?"

Tom paused and looked squarely at the presiding judge. "I would earnestly beseech of you, my lord," he continued, "when the passions and prejudices of this hour have passed, to appeal to your conscience. You may deem this language unbecoming, and perhaps it may seal my fate. But I must speak the truth as I know the truth, whatever its cost. I stand here regretting nothing I have ever done, retracting nothing I have ever said. I do not stand here to beg, with a lying lip, for the life I have consecrated to my country. Far from it. Even here—here where the thief, the libertine and the murderer have left their footprints in the dust, here where the shadows of death surround me—even here, encircled by these terrors, the hope which had beckoned me to my perilous position still consoles, animates and enraptures me."

His voice was now quaking with emotion, but Thomas Meagher went on, his shoulders square, defiance in his eyes. "Judged by the law of England, this crime entails the penalty of death. I knew that. But the history of Ireland explains my crime, if crime it be, and justifies it. Judged by that history, I am no criminal. I deserve no punishment. Judged by that history, the treason of which I stand convicted loses all its guilt, becomes sanctified as a duty, ennobled as a sacrifice. So, my Lord Chief Justice, pronounce the sentence. I am prepared to meet its execution. And I hope that I will be able to appear before a higher tribunal where a judge of infinite goodness and justice presides, and where, my lord, many of the judgments of this court, and this world, will be reversed."

It was a bold, brave attempt to let the world know the

full injustice of England to Ireland, since there were newspapermen from outside Great Britain in the courtroom. There was, however, no wild outburst from the jammed courtroom. A hush had settled over the large room, as if all in attendance had just heard a great sermon in a cathedral.

The Lord Chief Justice cleared his throat embarrassedly to break the silence, then read the sentence. "The sentence," he intoned, "is that you, Thomas Francis Meagher, be returned to Kilmainham Prison and from there be drawn on a hurdle to the place of execution, to be hanged by the neck until you are dead. And that afterward your head shall be severed from your body, and your body be divided into four quarters to be disposed of as Her Majesty sees fit. May God have mercy on your soul."

The most Thomas Meagher had hoped for from his presentence statement was that the world would perhaps exert influence on England and so secure future freedom for Ireland. In that he was wrong. But the newspapers of America, France, Germany and other European nations did rise to his defense. Criticisms of English policy, of British vengeance against one who fought for his own people, were spread around the globe.

England was embarrassed. Within three days Queen Victoria commuted the death sentence to transportation for life to Tasmania, then called Van Dieman's Land, an island off the southeastern tip of Australia.

Before seven the morning of July 10, 1849, Thomas Francis Meagher, with other exiled Irish patriots, was rushed aboard the *Swift,* a ten-gun warship. Soon the brig weighed anchor and started through St. George's Channel into the Atlantic.

Tom Meagher, in chains, looked out across the blue waters to see his homeland fading in the mist of morning.

VI
THE BOTTOM
OF THE WORLD

About fifteen thousand miles were covered by the *Swift* in transporting the Irish prisoners to Tasmania, south through the Atlantic and around the Cape of Good Hope. Only one stop was made, that at Simonstown near the cape.

The lengthy trip to the bottom of the world was not uncomfortable for Tom Meagher. None of the prisoners was badly treated. The captain of the *Swift*, though English, was considerate and kind to the Irish rebels. He did not keep the prisoners in chains and allowed them to walk the deck freely.

"No more than two at one time will be allowed on deck," he had said, in detailing the restrictions. "And you will not speak to any member of the ship's crew other than myself or the ship's doctor."

The moments he spent alone became torture for Tom. It was then, his mind in a turmoil, that he would search his memory for the one thing done wrong, the element

77

that had brought such utter confusion and turned freedom for all Ireland into confinement for life for a few.

The *Swift* had sailed due east from the Cape of Good
Hope, crossing the southern reaches of the Indian Ocean,
considered by many to be part of the Antarctic. Thomas
Meagher was on deck the afternoon of October 28, 1849,
when the southwest tip of Van Dieman's Land was first
sighted.

Tom was familiar with the history of Van Dieman's
Land. (It would not be named Tasmania until another
four years had passed, in 1853, when England would also
be persuaded to end transportation to the island and
send no more convicts.) The island had been discovered
in November 1642 by the greatest of Dutch navigators,
Abel Janszoon Tasman. A few months before, Tasman
had also discovered New Zealand under the sponsorship
of Anton Van Dieman, governor-general of the Dutch
East Indies.

Great Britain, having taken possession of eastern Australia in 1770 and established a penal colony at Botany
Bay near present-day Sydney in 1788, was determined to
control the entire area. Van Diemen's Land was separated
from Australia only by shallow Bass Strait, so England
moved in and took possession of the territory in 1803. In
1840 she also took over both North and South Islands of
New Zealand, again freezing out the Dutch.

Like Australia and New Zealand, Van Diemen's Land
was first utilized as a detention station for prisoners. It
was the simplest way to populate the area and maintain
control. By the time Thomas Meagher arrived, the original inhabitants of the island had been driven away.

The *Swift* swung around the southern tip of the island and steamed north about fifty miles to the harbor of Hobart Town, the capital. There the man in charge of assigning prisoners brought to the island came aboard to outline the conditions of their imprisonment.

"You will be separated," he told Meagher and the other convicted men. "No two of you will be allowed in the same area. However, I am pleased to report that each of you will be granted a ticket of leave."

The ticket of leave, he explained, gave each of the men almost complete freedom to move about the district to which he was assigned. They could live as they wished, with no restrictions on their movements or activities. Thomas Meagher breathed easier. It was far more than he expected.

"There are certain conditions, however," the man continued. "You must have conducted yourselves properly, causing no trouble, throughout the trip from Ireland to Hobart Town. The assurance of the captain on this point will be sufficient."

None of the men had any fears. Tom knew that the captain was a fair and compassionate man, and none of them had caused him a moment's concern.

"And there is one other, most important, condition," the man went on. "Each of you will be required to give an oath, as a man of honor, that you will not use the freedom granted by the ticket of leave as a means to attempt escape."

Tom felt as sure of the others as he was of himself. As unjust as he deemed the punishment which brought him to Van Diemen's Land, he knew that once he gave his word, as long as he was free under this ticket of leave, he would not try to escape. And what good was there in not pledging his word? With the wide Indian Ocean to the west and the even broader Pacific to the east—and fifteen thousand miles separating them from home— where could they find escape?

Thomas Meagher and all but two of the other Irishmen gave their word. The pair who refused were assigned to a camp on an island off the mainland in the Pacific, seventy miles north of Hobart Town. John Riley and Bruce Casey, Meagher's two closest friends among the prisoners, and two who had received lesser sentences than life, were allowed to remain in districts near the coast. Riley was assigned to Hobart and Casey to New Norfolk, a few miles north of Hobart Town, on the Derwent River.

Meagher was sent to Campbell Town, inland forty miles from the Pacific in the center of the island. The district in which he could move about as he pleased, live where he liked, was thirty-five miles wide, north to south, and fifteen miles east to west.

Meagher settled in a small village near Campbell Town. His father had provided him with sufficient money to more than care for his needs. The first few months there was little he could do beyond walking through the district and along the Macquarie River, or remaining in his small rented house to read.

In a short time he made friends and learned to enjoy what he considered a most pleasant pastime. He would ride a horse through the brush and forests in the district, hunting the padmelon, a type of kangaroo hardly larger than a fox terrier—a stocky little animal whose head was small in proportion to its body.

By accident one day, riding along near the southern extremity of the district he was allowed to roam, he discovered a small log hut occupied by a man named Cooper, a lonely and friendly hermit. The little cabin was located at the lower tip of Lake Sorell, in the foothills of the Great Western Mountains which ranged through the center of the island. Tom came again and again to see Cooper, to sit and talk and relieve his boredom.

Tom had arrived this day to find Cooper gone, the hut empty. He tied his horse to a post and walked along the shore of the lake for a short distance. He stopped near the point beyond which he could not travel without violating his pledge to remain in his own district. A few feet away stood a man, looking out across the water.

When the man turned, Tom gave a shout of surprise. He had expected the man might be Cooper. Instead, it was his friend Bruce Casey, who had been living in New Norfolk.

"And what—" both men shouted the same words at the same moment. They stopped and laughed loudly.

As it turned out, Casey was waiting for John Riley to come up from Hobart Town. No, neither had violated his pledge. As luck would have it, the three districts came to a common point at that spot on Lake Sorell. Each of the three could stand in his own district and converse with the others.

Riley soon made his appearance and all had a laugh at their good fortune. Meagher and Casey had only twenty miles to travel to the newfound rendezvous. Riley had to come almost thirty. From that day on they met every week, leaving their respective homes so as to arrive at Lake Sorell about the same time. Then they would sit and talk, exchanging information, each always remaining in his own district. They would have dinner together every visit, first one and then another bringing the food and cooking it over an open fire, passing plates across the boundary point.

At one of these scheduled get-togethers in May of 1850, Thomas Meagher received another surprise. John Riley rode in with a fourth friend, John Mitchel. Mitchel, the firebrand, had preceded the others into exile, and had been sent to Australia. In April he had been transferred to Hobart Town in Van Diemen's Land. Though only thirty-five, his health had suffered greatly. The authorities in Hobart had permitted him to live with the nearest prisoner, Riley.

It was a great reunion for Tom. Though he and Mitchel had at one time differed in their means of achieving Irish freedom, they had always respected each other. Tom was happy to see, as their weekly meetings went on with Mitchel now always making a fourth, that the patriot's health was slowly improving.

Before Christmas that year Tom met Mary Bennett, the daughter of a farmer in the district. She was everything he could hope for. She, in turn, found twenty-seven-year-old Thomas Meagher a man who suited her own dreams of a husband. They were married on February 22, 1851.

It was a mutually happy union. Tom, ecstatic about his new bride, built a small house on the shores of Lake

Sorell and prepared to live out his life exiled in Van Diemen's Land. It was an idyllic existence there on the shores of the beautiful lake with the towering mountains in the background, and little to do. But it was not long before Tom became morose and restless.

"What is it, Tom?" Mary asked him one morning. She had watched him for weeks as his enthusiasm for life seemed to decrease by the day. "Can it be you are tired of me so soon?"

Tom drew her close and kissed her warmly. "No! Never! " he said. "But I fear this is not the life I had hoped for the one I love so dearly. I am no farmer, and my insides churn to be doing something. If we could only leave Van Diemen's Land. If I could only take you somewhere where I can put meaning into my life, give you the good things you deserve!"

"I have seen you become sadder by the day," his wife told him, "and it grieves me greatly. Whatever you wish to do, that I also wish. But what is there?"

"I don't know, my love. I know only that nights I dream I have gone to a land where a useful and honorable career is open to me."

"You cannot return to Ireland or any of the British lands."

"No," Tom said sadly. "Though to see the green isle even just once more—" He stopped and thought. "Mary, my darling," he said finally. "If I should escape, would you follow me?"

"I will go with you from the start, Thomas Meagher!" she exclaimed.

"If only it could be done that way," he groaned. "But

it would be possible to make an escape only if I were alone."

"But I know you, my husband," Mary Meagher said. "You renewed your ticket of leave only in April. With such an unjust sentence as you received, I don't know why you should care. Yet I know that you would not violate your oath."

"Sadly, that is true," Tom admitted. "But if I returned my ticket of leave, would I not be free of my pledge?"

As the weeks and months flew by, Tom Meagher became more restless and more disturbed. On the one hand, his exile and the lack of opportunity to do anything meaningful drove him to plan escape. On the other, his love for his wife made any time away from her an agony. Day after day he mentally debated his problem, swaying from one course to the other. Finally, in December, he made a firm decision. He would have to escape.

He did not immediately mention his determination to Mary. There were many factors that had to be resolved, some not the least bit simple. Where he would ultimately settle was easily decided upon. It had to be the United States of America, the only true cradle of liberty, he was convinced, in the entire world. How to get there was the seemingly unsolvable problem. For this he needed clearer minds than his own.

Tom discussed the matter with John Mitchel, Bruce Casey and John Riley.

"America is your safest choice," Mitchel told him. "I have had it in mind myself. When I am back in full good health, I will find some means to reach San Francisco in the American West."

"Leaving your district will be no difficulty," Bruce Casey said. "But you must choose the direction with care."

"They will search first along the east coast, expecting you will cross the short route through the Pacific," Riley offered.

John Mitchel thought a moment. "Perhaps your safest route will be to make your way north to Bass Strait. It is the farthest to travel, but also the least likely. Riley and I can quietly make arrangements for a ship to pick you up from one of the small islands in the strait. But what of your ticket of leave?"

"I will surrender it before I leave my home," Tom said.

"I feared that would be your answer," Mitchel said. "Sometimes it does not pay to be an honorable man."

When they met again three days later, Mitchel was jubilant.

"It is all settled, Tom," he announced. "Here is the plan."

Meagher, when he was ready to leave, would ride away with two trustworthy men Mitchel had secured as guides. They would go northwest to the furthest tip of Van Diemen's Land, where a small fishing boat would transport Meagher to a small, uninhabited island in Bass Strait. A ship bound for Brazil would pick Tom up the following morning.

The two guides would arrive at Meagher's home on Lake Sorell the evening of January 3. The schedule of his escape had been planned around his departure from home no later than noon on the fourth.

Before noon the morning of January 3 a letter was handed the chief of the police detachment at the headquarters of the district in which Meagher had been confined. It notified the magistrate that Thomas Meagher was surrendering his ticket of leave as of the morning of January 4. It also stated that, if any attempt was made to arrest him before that time, he would consider himself as having been automatically released from his pledge.

Tom did not deceive himself in believing that the police would wait. He felt sure an arrest attempt would be made quickly and prepared himself accordingly. Late in the afternoon he told Mary of his decision and explained the plan to her.

"When I have arrived in Pernambuco," he told her, "I will send a letter to John Mitchel. You can then begin making arrangements to leave Van Diemen's Land to meet me in New York, for that is where I intend to go in America. There are many loyal Irish there."

Tom remained with Mary, expecting to hear momentarily that the police were on their way. After supper the two guides made their appearance. An hour later, as they sat chatting over a glass of wine, they heard the pound of speeding hoofbeats. Tom ran to the door. He was advised that the police were enroute to arrest him.

As the guides rushed out to saddle their horses, Tom kissed his wife goodbye and quickly repeated his instructions to her. He then mounted his horse, joining the two guides who were waiting. They rode off a few hundred feet and hid in tall brush. Within a half hour three constables rode up to the Meagher home and went inside.

"Wait here," Tom told his guides.

Carefully and quietly he guided his horse to within a few feet of the door.

"Here I am!" he shouted so the police could hear. "I'm Thomas Meagher, the man you came to arrest!"

The constables rushed out of the house.

"Catch me if you can!" Tom shouted and spurred his horse.

In a moment he had disappeared into the brush, and was joined by his two guides. They rode off north, concealed by the dense foliage. The constables, surprised by Tom's action, were caught unawares. By the time they mounted their horses, they were uncertain as to which direction to take. Meagher and his guides had made their escape with ease.

It took the three men a day and a half to reach the northwest coast of Van Diemen's Land. As they approached the end of their ride, they could see a small fishing boat waiting on the shore. Two young fishermen stood beside it.

At the shore Tom bid his guides good-bye. They wished him luck, then rode off. The two fishermen had the boat ready, and when Tom entered, they immediately rowed out into the waters of Bass Strait. The island on which Tom was to wait for his ship was only four miles off the mainland, but the sea was choppy and wild. The trip across those few miles took more than an hour. As they reached the bank, Tom turned to thank the fishermen and bid them good-bye.

"No, not now," the one man said. "If something should

happen and your ship does not arrive, you would be marooned with no way to reach the mainland. We will wait with you."

They erected a tentlike shelter in which to sleep. The next morning the three pairs of eyes scanned the seas for sight of sails. There was none. Nor was there any sign of a ship throughout the day. Throughout the next day it was more of the same—waiting, waiting, for a ship that did not arrive.

Tom's impatience turned to worry. What if there was to be no ship? It might have lost its way among the many islands dotting Bass Strait, anchored at the wrong one and then sailed away. He could not return to Lake Sorell without being arrested and confined in a detention camp.

The two fishermen, both patient, helped keep him from complete despair. "The ship is only delayed," they told him. "The waters are mean and wild in January. It takes time, much time."

Four days passed with no sign of the ship. Their provisions ran out, but the two fishermen refused to leave. "There are fish and birds' eggs," they pointed out. "We will not starve."

Day followed lonely day for Thomas Meagher, his hope ebbing further with each hour. He could not remain still, but walked along the rocky shore back and forth, scanning the horizon, waiting, hoping against hope.

On the eighth day, while the two fishermen were inland searching for eggs, Tom fell asleep. He was awakened by the sound of gunfire. Jumping up, he looked out into the water. There was a ship! It had sailed in as close as it could to shore and the captain, hugging the rigging, was waving a white cloth. It was his ship, Tom knew. The white cloth was the signal.

The two fishermen had heard the gunfire and had rushed back. Now they rowed Tom out to the ship, bid him good-bye and good luck and started for their home. Thomas Meagher stood on the deck of the *Elizabeth Thompson* as it hoisted sail, thanking God for the kindness and compassion of strangers. In a few minutes the *Elizabeth Thompson* was under way, moving out of Bass Strait into the Indian Ocean.

It was a tiring, tedious journey, but Thomas Meagher felt only exhilaration. He was free at last! The ship sailed past the Cape of Good Hope and into the wide Atlantic. He was closer to a good life. He began to plan for the future.

America would be his home for as long as Ireland was controlled by the English. But one day, he was sure, his people would rise again. He would be ready then to return and help in its final fight for liberty. Meanwhile, he could not wait to reach Brazil so that he might write his letters. There would be one to John Mitchel, signed with an agreed-upon alias in case the authorities were watching Mitchel's mail. In that he would give Mary the word to begin planning to meet him in New York. And he would write his father, begging him to leave Ireland and meet him on the free side of the Atlantic.

The *Elizabeth Thompson* docked at Pernambuco

(now called Recife), on the east coast of Brazil, in mid-March. The trip from Bass Strait had taken nine weeks. Thomas Meagher remained in Pernambuco only three days, then boarded an American brig, the *Alcorn*, and was on his way to New York.

VII
HOME OF THE BRAVE

The *Alcorn,* with Thomas Francis Meagher aboard, docked at New York on March 26, 1852. For the first time after his four years of exile, Tom felt really free. He knew that he had come to a country that had warmly welcomed many others like himself, that here in New York he would find many of his friends who had fled the miseries of Ireland under British rule.

Tom quickly found that he was not unexpected. Word of his escape from Tasmania had come across the Atlantic, and once the Irish of New York heard that he was coming to America, they made plans to honor him for the great Irish patriot he was.

As he stood on the pier, wondering which way to turn, he was surprised to hear his name shouted. He turned to find Michael Cavanaugh, whom he had known well in Ireland and who had escaped to New York long before, running toward him.

Cavanaugh called out as he ran, "Tom! Tom Meagher!"

Tom was stunned. How could anyone have known that he was aboard the *Alcorn,* much less that he would arrive at that moment? His face revealed his astonishment.

"Come now!" Cavanaugh laughed. "It's not a ghost you see, and rest your blessed mind. I was here on the pier only by accident, and there you were."

"But how could you remember me, Michael?" Tom asked when the mutually warm greetings were finished. "I was a young lad when last we saw each other."

"Sixteen, perhaps seventeen, but such a lad!" Cavanaugh shook his head, a sly grin on his face.. "With a mien one could never forget. As Irish as the hills of Killarney, straight and strong, laughing blue eyes—and still they sparkle—and dark brown curly hair. No, there was no mistaking the figure standing there. It's Tom Meagher, and no one else, I said to myself!"

"You look well yourself, Michael Cavanaugh," Tom remarked. "America has treated you well."

"Praise be!" Cavanaugh said. "But not half so well as it will treat the greatest of Ireland's heroes."

If anything, Michael Cavanaugh had understated the welcome New York gave Thomas Meagher. His arrival was an occasion of widespread rejoicing and celebrating, especially for the Irish. The newspapers heralded his arrival in glowing terms. He was received enthusiastically wherever he went, tendered invitations to public dinners and receptions. He accepted none until, embarrassed, he could not refuse a banquet in his honor planned by the city of New York at the Astor House on June 10.

"While my country remains in sorrow and subjection," he told the audience of officials and others that night in explanation of his refusals, "it would be indelicate of me to participate in the many festivities offered me. When she lifts her head and nerves her arm for a bolder struggle—when she goes forth like Miriam, with song and timbrel, to celebrate her victory—I, too, shall lift up my head and join in the hymn of freedom."

There was a second invitation Meagher could not refuse. This was to review the annual Fourth of July parade of the New York National Guard. That day he stood on the reviewing stand overlooking Broadway. Thousands of New Yorkers lined the flag-draped street as Tom stood at attention while the colors of the precision-marching regiments of the Guard passed by.

Not only the National Guard units participated in the parade. There were the volunteer fire brigades, fife and drum corps, fraternal societies, military bands in great number and regular army regiments from the forts surrounding New York. And, of course, with so many of his countrymen in New York, there were countless Irish in the parade, particularly in the police and fire battalions.

As the Stars and Stripes passed before the reviewing stand, Thomas Meagher experienced an emotional upsurge he had felt before only at the sight of the Irish flag. Then, later, as the band played the Star-Spangled Banner and the crowd sang its words, he again felt his throat go dry and his chest tighten. Throughout the balance of the afternoon, and into the evening, two phrases he had heard sung haunted his mind: "Land of the free" and "Home of the Brave." This, he thought, is what I had dreamed of for Ireland. And this, he was now convinced, was his country—at least until Ireland had gained its freedom.

That evening Michael Cavanaugh came to him. "Tom," he said, "after the parade today a few of us were talking. All had seen you on the reviewing stand and seemed to read your eyes. There was a fire in them and pride."

Tom nodded. "I felt both," he said. "Proud to be here in America, and at the same time wishing we had such strong fighting Irish back home."

"Which is why I am here," Cavanaugh explained. "We who have been here three years or more have been proud of our people, proud they have become Americans as well as Irish and have become organized into fine fighting groups. You saw that for yourself."

"Indeed I did."

"So in talking this afternoon we wondered if perhaps we might call all the Irish in New York to a great meeting. Would you talk to them?"

"Could I do less?" Tom asked.

"Thank you, Tom," Cavanaugh said. "It will be of great help in making us even more unified. We will have a review of the militia groups first, then a dinner in the evening at Castle Garden."

The affair was held on July 27. Thomas Meagher reviewed the Irish battalions in Battery Park and later addressed the assemblage in Castle Garden. He devoted the best part of his talk to the freedom and the sanctuary granted the Irish in the United States.

"Under this star-filled flag," he told the crowd, "the poorest shop keeper, the poorest artisan is cheered by the thought that he, no less than the wealthiest, is an active and equal part of the government—that by his vote he directs its officials, and by his arms, and the habits they impose, helps in defending his country."

What he had seen in America during the two and a half months since he left the *Alcorn* excited Thomas Meagher. He decided it must be his country whether or not he ever returned to fight for Ireland. On August 9, 1852, he stood before the clerk in New York's Superior Court and took the oath of intent to become a citizen of the United States.

The following day he wrote to Ireland asking his wife to come to America. She, too, had finally escaped from Tasmania to Waterford, and was waiting there for word from Tom. She and Tom's father were to come to New York together.

Thomas Meagher now began accepting invitations to speak. Colorful, eloquent and exciting, he quickly became one of the most distinguished lecturers of the time. He spoke in all the large cities of the North and then made a tour of the South.

Entertained lavishly in all the Southern cities he visited, he learned to love the calm, serene life he saw. The pastoral beauty of Virginia reminded him of Ireland, and the Old World charm of New Orleans brought back memories of Paris. At the conclusion of his first extended lecture tour he returned to New York in January 1853.

In the spring Tom's wife Mary arrived from Ireland accompanied by her companion and friend, Eloise Riley, and Tom's father. The first few months after her arrival he would accept no lecture engagements. There was so much of America he wanted her to see.

They visited the Catskills, Lakes George and Champlain, Niagara Falls. They walked through New York City from the Battery north to the wilds of what would become Central Park in a few years, and east and west between the Hudson and East Rivers, and across into Brooklyn. They were happy days for both Tom and Mary.

Early in September Tom, Mary and Eloise Riley were at dinner in the Meagher home on East Twenty-third Street.

"I am glad that you are here, Eloise," Tom said.

"I am glad that you were kind enough to have me," she answered. "But I know there is a reason you say it now."

"I need not be told," Mary put in. "I saw the letters about your lecture in San Francisco. But will that keep you long?"

"I have heard much of that city," Eloise said. "It is thousands of miles from New York."

"Which is why I am happy you are here to keep Mary company," Tom said. "I will be leaving in two weeks and be gone perhaps two months."

Before Tom could leave for San Francisco, his wife

was taken sick. He began to worry about her remaining in New York through the bitter winters he had already experienced.

"Perhaps it would be better if we returned to Ireland for the winter," Eloise told him. "The bad days there are mild."

"You are right, Eloise," Tom told her. "Say nothing yet to Mary until I make the arrangements. It would be better for her in a mild climate. And Father will be glad to have you both. He must be lonesome since he returned home."

Thomas Meagher was never to see his wife again. In May a letter from his father told him that Mary had died giving birth to a son. Eloise Riley, the elder Meagher wrote Tom, would care for the boy in his home until he was grown and able to join him in New York.

Early in 1854 John Mitchel arrived, another exile escapee from Tasmania. Typical of Mitchel, he came to New York with great plans.

"I am going to publish a newspaper," he told Tom. "The world must know that Irish people in Ireland are not so weak as to be loyal to Queen Victoria. Nor have those of us who came to America, or went to Australia or New Zealand, been satisfied in accepting defeat."

"What will this paper be?" Tom asked.

"It will come out weekly and be called *The Citizen,*" Mitchel answered. "And I want you to help me."

Meagher agreed and began writing regular articles for *The Citizen.* He also continued his public speaking. In the written as well as the spoken word, his fiery expressions and messages of hope for the future helped lift the spirits of Irish people everywhere.

Thomas Meagher now began to consider the American political scene seriously. He had seen a great change come about since his arrival in New York. Great men in the American Congress—Webster, Clay, Calhoun, names he had come to revere—had died or retired from active life. Now the names he heard were those of Jefferson Davis, Stephen Douglas, William H. Seward. And, to a lesser degree, that of a somewhat obscure Illinois lawyer named Abraham Lincoln.

Stephen Douglas, in 1854, introduced the Kansas-Nebraska bill in Congress. The bill would take the matter of slavery away from the jurisdiction of the House and Senate and make it a local matter, to be decided upon by the citizens of the individual states. Not merely trouble brewed as a result, but also murders and massacres.

The Republican Party, which evolved from the short-lived Free-Soil group opposing slavery, was gaining strength. In 1856, though the Democrats, with James Buchanan as their Presidential candidate, won, the Republicans took eleven of fifteen Northern states. The danger signals were clear. Southern leaders became emphatic. The election of a Republican President would definitely drive them out of the Union.

Thomas Meagher's sympathies were with the South in those early days of turmoil. He had likened their plight—though he detested the thought of slavery—to that of

Ireland: a people being subjected by another to policies they did not believe in. But he was kept too busy the early months of 1856 to join the issue.

In May he remarried. He had met a New York girl, Elizabeth Townsend, six months after Mary's death. And he was studying law, finally being admitted to the New York bar. About the same time he founded a newspaper of his own, *The Citizen* having ceased to exist when John Mitchel left for San Francisco to live. Meagher's paper, the *Irish News,* continuing the principles of the paper published jointly by him and Mitchel, was an immediate success.

After two years of editing the *Irish News,* growing restless and bored from lack of action, he assigned management of the paper to his assistant. *Harper's* Magazine offered to send him to Central America to do a series of travel articles. He readily assented. Meagher enjoyed the travel and the visits to new countries, but when he returned to New York in the fall of 1860, he was happy to be back. And he found himself embroiled in a near international incident.

While he was on his way back from Central America, the Prince of Wales, eldest son of Queen Victoria, had visited New York during a tour of the United States. A mammoth parade was arranged for the prince. The New York National Guard was ordered to march in the parade. Michael Corcoran, a general in the Fenian Brotherhood, an Irish revolutionary society, as well as a colonel in the Guard, held back the Irish regiment he commanded, the

New York 69th. He could not allow his Irish to participate in a tribute to the son of the hated queen who had
brought such suffering to their people.

Meagher was back in New York as the storm over Corcoran's action broke. The colonel was castigated by the
New York papers, accused of an insult to the English flag
and of precipitating possible war with England. In his
Irish News Meagher defended Corcoran.

"Lawfully as a citizen, courageously as a soldier, indig-
nantly as an Irishman," he wrote in his colorful prose,
"Colonel Corcoran refused to parade his stalwart Irish
in honor of the beardless youth who, succeeding to the
spoils of the Tudors and Stuarts, is destined one day to
wield the scepter that has been the scourge of Ireland."

Until that time, though he had been outspoken in his
loyalty and love for Ireland, and his hatred of the British ·
for the starvation, evictions, persecutions and injustices,
Thomas Meagher had not considered joining the militant
Fenian Brotherhood. Now he did not hesitate. He felt it
necessary to prove where his loyalties truly lay. He joined
the Fenians.

Simultaneous with Thomas Meagher's decision to take
a more active part in Irish protests, the political climate
in the United States was moving toward a stormy peak.
Abraham Lincoln was elected as the Presidential nominee
of the Republican Party. The Democrats, split into
Northern and Southern contingents, nominated two men,
Stephen Douglas by the North and John Breckinridge,
Buchanan's Vice-President, by the South. Lincoln, carry-

ing every Northern state, was elected with 180 electoral votes to Breckinridge's 72. Now there was no more compromise. The sad hour of disunion had come.

South Carolina, the leader in Southern political philosophy, was first to go. It did not wait for Lincoln's inauguration. Its legislature, summoned into special session on December 20, 1860, voted to secede. In January and February, the Gulf States—the Southern rim of the United States, spanning all the states from Florida and Georgia to Texas—followed suit. Delegates from all the states met at Montgomery, Alabama, and there set up the provisional government of the Confederate States of America. Jefferson Davis of Mississippi was elected President. The more northerly of the Southern states, Virginia, North Carolina, Tennessee and Arkansas, had not yet seceded.

The Confederacy had stolen a march on the Union in another way as well. Almost every fort in the South was taken over by the Confederacy as Southern generals surrendered them with all their arms and supplies. At only a few did officers, remaining loyal, refuse to give up. One of these was Fort Sumter in the harbor of Charleston, South Carolina.

Lincoln took office with the bomb of war already detonated and ready to explode. He waited quietly and patiently, hoping to give men's passions time to cool. Finally, he had to make at least one vital move. The garrison at Fort Sumter needed supplies. Food was getting short since they were barricaded inside the fort and surrounded by the hostile South. Lincoln notified South Carolina that he was sending help to the soldiers at Sumter.

Charleston had already set up a ring of batteries around the fort. On April 12, 1861, they opened fire, hoping to compel Fort Sumter to surrender before the supplies could arrive. Major Anderson, commanding Sumter, withstood two days of cannonading. Then, his ammunition exhausted and the fort on fire, he surrendered. The Civil War was under way.

In New York, Meagher, who had repeatedly told friends his sympathies were with the South, read about the assault on Sumter in horror. The flag has been fired upon. That was his only thought.

"Damn them!" he exploded. "Damn them that did not let the flag alone!"

Elizabeth, his wife, had been in the next room of their home when she heard the outburst. She rushed into the library where Tom still held the paper, staring at it with fire in his eyes.

"Tom!" she exclaimed. "Does this mean you will join the army?"

He looked up at her. "What else can I do?" he asked. "There is no other course I can take. They have fired on my flag. It is my duty as a patriot. It is the duty of every Irishman who has found liberty in America to defend the country which gave us a new home."

VIII
DEBACLE AT
MANASSAS JUNCTION

Just as the assault on the Stars and Stripes over Fort Sumter decided Thomas Meagher's course, so, too, it unified the North. Democratic Senator Douglas, defeated by Lincoln and an outspoken critic of his policies, pledged his full support. Everywhere the reaction was the same. The flag had been assailed, so there was nothing to do but fight.

With the North girding its belt and preparing for war, the South drew closer together. The remaining Southern states, put in the position of fighting their neighbors, joined them instead. The same Virginia convention which weeks before voted for union, now voted to secede, an action which placed its most distinguished son in a most difficult position.

Robert E. Lee, a great soldier and officer, a Virginian who loved the Union with a passion, made the most difficult choice of a lifetime. He could not, in conscience, do other than remain loyal to his state. He left the United

States Army to become military adviser to Jefferson Davis.

Other slave states quickly followed Virginia's lead—only Delaware, Maryland, Missouri, and Kentucky remained loyal.

Three days after Sumter, Lincoln asked for seventy-five thousand volunteers. He made it clear that his cause was not an attack on slavery, but rather the putting down of an armed assault upon the Union. The North responded wholeheartedly and enthusiastically.

New York's quota was thirteen thousand men. The total was quickly reached. The 69th Regiment of the New York State militia was one of the first to respond, over-enrolling its one-thousand-men limit by over two thousand. This was the same 69th, commanded by Colonel Michael Corcoran, which weeks before had refused to parade in honor of England's Prince of Wales. It did not hesitate when the call came to offer its services on the field of battle in defense of the Constitution. Its exclusively Irish membership itched for the chance to help their adopted country.

April 23, 1861, was the day scheduled for the departure of the 69th Regiment. It seemed to Thomas Meagher as though the entire Atlantic coast had come to New York to bid the Irish Brigade good luck. From early morning great crowds began flocking into Broadway, along the route of the parade.

The day was blistering hot for April. A bright sun shone down on colorful banners and bunting, warming the hearts of men, women and children who had converged on the Great White Way from Hoboken, Brooklyn, Newark and as far away as Hartford, Connecticut.

Thomas Meagher had joined the contingent of the 69th known as the Phoenix Zouaves. They had been so honored by his choosing them that they had unanimously elected him their commander, with the rank of captain. In the Zouave uniform, Tom cut a dashing figure. He wore baggy trousers, a tight black coat and hat curled up at the side, and he rode a handsome white horse leading the Zouaves, all similarly dressed except for the difference in trouser color—some bright red, some bright green, some black.

The march began from the headquarters of the 69th Regiment in Prince Street. It proceeded to Broadway with the bands of the fire companies and police serenading them as they passed. Excitement built higher as they passed Canal, Grand and then Cortlandt Streets, finally to arrive at the pier where the steamer *James Adger* waited to carry them as far as Annapolis, Maryland.

With the shouts of thirty thousand splitting the April air, the *James Adger* began moving away. A band struck up "The Wearing of the Green." A cannon was fired. The Irish Brigade was off to the wars!

On their arrival in Annapolis, Colonel Corcoran, as commander of the Regiment, received orders to take his men through Baltimore and Washington and across the Potomac River into Virginia. Leaving the steamer, the men massed into formation and began the long march—first through Baltimore and then into the nation's capital, where they swept by the half-finished new dome of the Capitol building.

Thomas Meagher had visited Washington before, but now there was a special thrill in passing the many government buildings, in guiding his beautiful white horse across the Potomac. He looked up at Arlington Heights where the white-columned home of Robert E. Lee stood etched against the afternoon sky. He turned to the man riding beside him and pointed to the mansion.

"We'll yet regret the man's loyalty to the South," he said in his still thick Irish brogue. "There is no finer man, or greater soldier, than Robert E. Lee."

The 69th Regiment was to assist in the defense of Washington. To save the nation's capital from invasion by Confederate troops massing around Richmond, Virginia, the new capital of the Confederacy, the Federals had to take and hold Arlington Heights. This was a ridge which extended about five miles on the Virginia side of the Potomac.

The commanding officer decided to deploy eight thousand men down the Potomac as far as Alexandria, Virginia. The 69th was to entrench and hold the hill beside the Aqueduct Bridge leading into Washington's Georgetown area.

Thomas Meagher and the Irish Brigade were dropped immediately into the area where heavy action from both sides was to be expected. The most important arena for battle, once Jefferson Davis had moved the Confederate capital from Alabama to Virginia, had to be the less than one hundred miles of sparsely populated plains, hills and woods that separated Washington and Richmond. It seemed as though the two capitals sat waiting, frowning defiantly across the miles at each other, the one daring the other to come and get it.

Because of its location, Washington was the more vulnerable. Situated as it was between Maryland and Virginia, both slave states—Maryland never did secede but her Confederate sympathies were strong—the capital was literally surrounded by hostile territory.

As volunteers began pouring into Washington, fear of the immediate seizure of the city was quieted. With its defense seemingly secure, impatience for action was felt throughout the North. From Boston to St. Louis the cry "On to Richmond" was being raised. Newspapers began clamoring against the slowness with which the Federal army was moving toward battle.

Forgotten in the impatience to get on with the war was the fact that a large proportion of the U.S. Army's officers had been Southern and had resigned, so that even the regulars were demoralized. The rest of Lincoln's troops were raw recruits who had answered the call for volunteers but were still in need of exhaustive training. This posed an almost insolvable problem for President Lincoln. He was, under the Constitution, commander-in-chief, but he openly admitted his military inexperience and was forced to depend on the judgment of his generals.

Jefferson Davis, as president of the Confederacy, held a broad military edge over Lincoln. He was a graduate of the military academy. He had commanded a regiment in the Mexican War with distinction. He had served as President Pierce's Secretary of War. As Senator from his home state of Mississippi until the outbreak of war, he also chaired the Military Affairs Committee of the United States Senate.

Unlike Lincoln, who had come to the Presidency as a comparative unknown, with little knowledge of the abilities of the officers of the army, Davis was an acknowledged, experienced leader. He knew intimately the backgrounds of his Southern officers, knew which were the most promising and the areas in which they could serve most effectively. Few of the men he appointed to commands were removed or replaced.

Thomas Meagher, studying the respective strengths of the two forces during the first days at Arlington Heights, was a bit disheartened at what seemed to be Southern superiority. Davis himself, he found, with Lee as his adviser, acted as his own military commander and strategist. His chief generals in Virginia were capable fighting men, Brigadier General Joseph E. Johnston and Brigadier General Pierre Beauregard, the latter a great hero of the moment for his capture of Fort Sumter.

On the Union side, Lincoln frankly admitting inexperience, important military decisions were in the hands of Lieutenant General Winfield Scott, supreme commander of the Union armies, now old and nearing the end of his military career. Actively in command of the Virginia forces was forty-three-year-old Irvin McDowell, until May 14 a major, but then promoted to brigadier general.

On June 3 General Scott ordered McDowell to prepare for a move toward Manassas Junction in an attempt to divert the Confederate forces. Meanwhile an attack would be made on Harper's Ferry, the scene of the John Brown incident, on the bluffs above the confluence of the Potomac and Shenandoah Rivers.

McDowell had been in command of the forces deployed along Arlington Heights for hardly a month. His untrained volunteers were anything but ready. Until the moment he received the directive from General Scott, he had had no intimation that any assault against the South was being planned. General Scott had also asked him to forward an estimate of the strength of the force he could provide for the attack at Manassas Junction, near a small stream called Bull Run, thirty miles southeast of Washington. McDowell advised Scott that he could furnish twelve thousand infantry, six or eight companies of cavalry, two batteries and a reserve force of five thousand men. He prepared to leave Arlington Heights and waited.

The news of possible action thrilled the men of the Irish Brigade who had been champing at the bit while digging trenches and drilling. Thomas Meagher, also impatient to get into action, was not so sure that they were ready for a concerted assault. The men still needed considerable training.

Orders for the move did not come. When Patterson, the general leading the Union troops toward Harper's Ferry, began his attack, Confederate General Johnston gave up Harper's Ferry. General Scott sent hurried orders to McDowell to remain where he was since there was now no need for a diversionary tactic.

Meagher breathed a sigh of relief. Any delay meant more time, and that in turn could mean saved lives. But he didn't reckon with the power of public outcry. Again throughout the North the "On to Richmond" cry was heard. The demand for some advance by the Union army became so clamorous that something had to be done. Orders were passed down.

The evening of July 15 the 69th Regiment was called to attention by Colonel Corcoran, with Thomas Meagher standing nearby as captain of the Zouaves. The men of the regiment stood tense, anticipating what was to come.

"The day is here, men," Colonel Corcoran announced. "We march tomorrow with General McDowell's army. May God bless and protect you all."

Temple Emmett, a lieutenant second in command to Meagher in the Zouaves, came to Tom when the formation was dismissed.

"Captain," Emmett said, "I'm afraid we are not ready for battle."

"My sentiments, Emmett," Meagher replied. "But as soldiers we go on and follow orders. Yet, as a man, I am concerned for my brave Zouaves. I can only hope that we return in the same numbers as we leave."

The following morning, as an integral part of General Irvin McDowell's force of fifty thousand, the 69th Regiment began its march south through Virginia. The Zouaves, led by Thomas Meagher, and all segments of the 69th were part of one column of soldiers commanded by General William T. Sherman. All the men in McDowell's force carried no more than three days' rations. The army was to be followed by provision wagons which would leave Alexandria the following day.

The advance the first day was without incident. It was expected that the Confederates would make a stand at Fairfax Court House, but before they approached the village the Confederates retreated.

"Is there to be no fighting?" Temple Emmett asked Meagher.

"For the sake of our untrained men, nothing would please me more," Meagher answered, his words a prayer.

The morning of July 18 McDowell's forces reached Centreville, about twenty miles inland from the Potomac and about two miles east of Bull Run. Again, as the Union army approached, General Beauregard led the Confederates away.

The small stream named Bull Run was midway between Centreville and the village of Manassas Junction. It was banked by quick-dropping ground, fringed by dense forest. Artificial defenses had been set up for eight miles, between Union Mills on the south and Stone Bridge on the north.

The little river itself could be forded, but every crossing in that eight-mile span was defended by one of Beauregard's contingents. McDowell, finding this situation, realized that his original hope of coming up on General Beauregard from the rear was out of the question. He ordered an encampment for all troops except a division under General Tyler to spread around Centreville.

Tyler, having misunderstood McDowell's instructions to him to "keep up the impression that we are moving on Manassas," pushed ahead from Centreville with one squadron of cavalry and two companies of infantry. His purpose was to reconnoiter Mitchell and Blackburn fords which were crossings to the direct road to Manassas Junction.

Arriving at the crest of the ridge which overlooks Bull Run, Tyler could see Beauregard's forces on the opposite bank of the river. He quickly ordered up two 20-pound rifle guns, a field battery of six guns and a brigade of infantry. The Union contingent opened fire from the ridge, exchanging only a few shots with the enemy batteries.

At four in the afternoon Sherman, commanding the Fourth Brigade of McDowell's army, the brigade which included the 69th regiment, received orders to move his men to the front. They were to relieve forces which had been under fire. Sherman assigned the duty to Colonel Corcoran of the 69th.

With the Irish flag fluttering in the breeze beside the Stars and Stripes, the 69th took off under a burning sun. In an hour they reached the ridge where Tyler's regiment was withstanding the shelling of Confederate batteries. Meigher and his Zouaves resumed the return fire on the enemy as the tired, withdrawing regiments took their well-earned rest. For the rest of the afternoon and into early evening they held the position but were unable to drive off the enemy. During the middle of the evening General McDowell rode up to examine the situation personally.

"It's too strong a position," he said to Colonel Corcoran. "It cannot be attacked successfully. Take your regiment back to Centreville."

The 69th, with the rest of McDowell's army, remained

at Centreville for two more days, a delay which proved of great benefit to the Confederates. Beauregard used the time to shift his forces, without McDowell's scouts being any the wiser. When General Johnston arrived at Manassas Junction on the twentieth and took command, the Confederates were more than merely solidly entrenched behind impregnable defenses. Their forces now outnumbered McDowell's army by over four thousand men.

McDowell now committed a fatal blunder. His plan was to deceive the enemy by feigning an assault on the Stone Bridge over Bull Run. Two columns would meanwhile make the actual attack on the Confederate left.

The Confederates were not deceived. When the Federals marched through the forest toward their left wing, they were ready. Despite this foreknowledge, when the attack came, the Confederates were momentarily repulsed and had to rush in reserve strength.

McDowell countered with additional Union troops, including the 69th Regiment. The fighting continued and the two forces came closer to each other until only the narrow river separated the fighters. When the New York regiment charged furiously at the Confederates, they forced a short retreat. It was at this point that General Jackson came with more reinforcements in gray.

Jackson and General Bee split into two groups, deploying their men in two areas. They resumed fire against the Union forces, Jackson rallying his men to return the charge. Seeing him, General Bee turned to an aide and said: "Look at General Jackson. He stands there like a

stone wall." And General Thomas Jackson became
known from that moment as "Stonewall" Jackson.

The Union army continued to struggle for position. By
the morning of July 21 they had gained no ground.
Weary and exhausted, they were now faced by an even
stronger Confederate force. Four thousand men had come
up to join Beauregard from the Shenandoah.

Overwhelmed, outnumbered, their dead scattered
along the banks of Bull Run, the Federals retreated,
leaving behind three thousand killed, wounded or captured. The Confederates had lost only two thousand.

When the last attack of the 69th Regiment was repulsed, Colonel Corcoran ordered them to withdraw to
the ford over which it had crossed Bull Run. Forced to
cross the river on a narrow wooden pathway they could
move only in a single column.

Most of the 69th had crossed the river in safety when
a shout was heard: "The enemy is coming!" The result
was confusion as the men started running and pushing
past each other. In the melee, while Corcoran and
Meagher tried to restore order to the retreat, the enemy
swooped down. Meagher, in front, was across the river in
time. Colonel Corcoran, at the rear of the regiment, was
captured by the Confederates.

With Michael Corcoran a prisoner, the 69th New
York was without a leader, but for only a short time. The
following morning the surviving officers of the regiment
named Thomas Meagher as their leader.

IX
THE FIGHTING IRISH

A week had passed since the clumsy failure at Bull Run. Thomas Meagher and his 69th were still at Fort Corcoran awaiting orders. The regiment's enlistment period was near expiration and the men were restless. Tom did his best to keep the men busy, wondering all the while what he should do.

True, the Confederates had dealt the Federals a crushing defeat and the South was jubilant. For them the war was all but over, won in a single skirmish. Yet, Tom thought, having learned his own sad lesson at Kilkenny, the Federals' approach to the battle had been too calm, too self-assured. It was a certainty that, now that they had tasted defeat, things would change. The gaunt, bearded man in the White House was not one to give up so easily.

"Look, Tom!" Lieutenant Brian McMahon said, coming up on Meagher as he sat wondering about the future. He was waving a copy of the London *Times*. "America's enemies are having a field day. England—and there are re-

ports out of Paris and Madrid in here, too—say our democratic institutions have all been proved rotten by the
defeat at Manassas Junction."

Tom took the paper and read the stories quickly. "What
else could one expect?" he said. "It is what they have
hoped for. And what more would an autocrat like Louis
Napoleon say but that self-government is impossible?"

"What do you think, Tom?" McMahon asked. "Can
the North recover from such losses as we had? Is Lincoln
strong enough to keep the Union together?"

"I cannot let myself think otherwise," Tom said. "A
great nation like this—one with a government and laws
that protects one such as I, who was not born here, equally
with those who were—such a nation cannot be allowed
to die."

At that moment a courier approached, saluted smartly
and handed Meagher a dispatch. Tom opened it and
scanned it quickly, as if knowing its contents in advance.

"It has come," he said, tapping the War Department
communiqué. "Our enlistment period has been completed. Have the sergeant major assemble the men right
away."

Within fifteen minutes Major Thomas Meagher was
addressing the men of the 69th Regiment. "I have just
received our orders," he called out. "The War Department has recognized the expiration of your three-month
enlistment period. We will break camp immediately and
begin our trip back to New York."

The return of the 69th Regiment to New York was a
thrilling experience for Thomas Meagher and his men.

The New York press had recounted their action at Manassas Junction in exciting phrases. It seemed that all Manhattan lined Broadway, cheering wildly, as the regiment paraded proudly before them.

Tom could not forget the reception they received. On arriving back in New York he had decided that he must fight on for his new country. He was ready to enlist in the regular army after a visit to a Washington hospital to see some of his men who had been wounded at Bull Run. Then the War Department offered him a commission as captain in the regulars.

Why he refused the commission, Tom was never certain. He had thanked the War Department, and suggested that there were many senior officers in the 69th who were more deserving of the honor. But that was not the primary reason. No, he thought, when he was back in New York, it was the warmth and cheerfulness of the injured Irish in the Washington hospital that had made him hesitate. He felt that he owed them something, had a debt to pay to those who had died at Bull Run, and those who had returned with him to New York. And how better to discharge that debt than by organizing an all-Irish brigade that would be attached as an integral part of the U.S. Army?

Once his mind was made up, Thomas Meagher didn't hesitate. He sent a telegram to the Secretary of War for authority to raise such a unit. Permission was received August 30, 1861. Brian McMahon, who had served as his first lieutenant in the 69th, was among the first to join Tom.

"Of course you will command the brigade," McMahon told Tom.

"No!" Tom exclaimed. "Of course not! The Irish Brigade should be commanded by General James Shields, if he'll accept."

Brigadier General James Shields was one of America's most renowned Irishmen, a great soldier turned statesman. He had earned an excellent military record in the Mexican War, had served in the United States Senate for six years from Illinois, and after moving to Minnesota in 1857, was appointed to fill out a one-year term from that state. A letter was immediately sent to Shields in California, offering him the command.

Thomas Meagher was determined to have the Irish Brigade well organized before Shields arrived. This meant hard work and long hours, and Tom threw himself into the organizational detail. Five regiments were to make up the Irish Brigade, with the 69th first. Two others would be organized in New York, the fourth in Pennsylvania and the fifth in Massachusetts. All three states were well populated with Irishmen. Tom would personally supervise recruitment for the New York regiments.

Headquarters for the Irish Brigade were established at 596 Broadway, above the Metropolitan Hotel, in a long, unattractive, uninspiring room, sparsely furnished with one desk, a solitary chair and a few benches. The bleak walls were decorated only with a few placards announcing that men could enroll there in the Irish Brigade. Yet a vibrancy and excitement pervaded that nearly bare room night and day, because Thomas Meagher all but lived there, his fiery personality giving it the aura of a royal court.

The New York papers gave wide coverage to the formation of the Irish Brigade. A steady stream of men entered the room above the Metropolitan Hotel on Broadway. Dunnigans and Mulligans, Flahertys and O'Connors, Kennedys and Caseys, McDonnells and McCarthys all came to join. It seemed to Tom that every possible clan from the auld sod was represented in New York and wanted to help their new country. And wherever he went, Thomas Meagher was his own best public-relations man. His speeches, rousing in their tone and provocative in their content, delivered in rich sincerity with a brogue reminiscent of the peat bogs and potato fields of home, never failed to stir men to action.

At Jones' Woods, New York, he spoke at a benefit for the survivors of those in the 69th who had given their lives at Bull Run. Seldom has anyone better expressed the significance of the battle to maintain the Union. He told the crowd:

"Never, I repeat, was there a cause more sacred, nor one more just, nor one more urgent. No cause more sacred, for it comprehends all that has been considered most desirable, most valuable, most ennobling to political society and humanity at large.

No cause more just, for it involves no scheme of conquest, or subjugation, contemplated no disfranchisement of the citizen, excluding the idea of provincialism and inferiority, aiming only at restoration of franchised powers and property, which were enjoyed by one people and one republic, and which, to be the means of happiness, fortune, and renown to millions, must be exercised and held in common under one code of national laws, one flag, and one executive.

No cause more urgent, for intrigues, perfidies, armed legions, the hatred and cupidity of foreign courts assail it; and every reverse with which it is visited serves as a pretext for the desertion of the coward, the misrepresentation of the politician, whose nation is his pocket."

He spoke on, outlining the benefits of liberty under the democracy of the American Constitution, contrasting it with the subjugation of peoples to the dictates of a monarch. "Will the Irishmen of New York," he went on, "stand by this cause—resolutely, heartily, with inexorable fidelity, despite all of the sacrifices it may cost, despite all of the dangers it may compel them, despite the bereavements and abiding gloom it may bring on such homes as this day miss the industry and love of the dead soldiers of the 69th . . . ?"

Cheers, shouts of "Yes" and "We will" echoed throughout the hall. Meagher continued:

"For my part, I ask no Irishman to do that which I myself am not prepared to do. My heart, my arm, my life are pledged to the national cause, and to the last it will be my highest pride, as I conceive it to be my holiest duty and obligation, to share its fortunes. I care not to what party the chief magistrate of the Republic has belonged. I care not upon which platform he may have been elected. That platform disappears before the Constitution, under the injunction of the oath he took on the steps of the Capitol the day of his inauguration. The party disappears in the presence of the nation—and as the chief magistrate, duly elected and duly sworn is bound to protect and administer the national property for the benefit of the nation, so should every citizen concur with him in loyal and patriotic action, discarding the mean persuasions and maxims of the local politician—and substituting the national interests, the national efficiency, the national honor, for the selfishness, the huckstering or the vengeance of a party."

The speech was hailed as the most definitive expression of the ideals and hopes on which the United States Constitution was founded. Reporters likened the words of Thomas Meagher to those of Washington and Jefferson. New York was stirred as never before. Its Irish population pointed proudly to Thomas Francis Meagher as one of their own, and men stormed the doors at 596 Broadway, quickly filling the three New York regiments of the Irish Brigade.

With New York recruitment so successful, Tom went to Boston to spur enrollment in the Massachusetts regiment. He spoke at a great meeting in the Boston Music Hall, presided over by Governor John A. Andrew of the Bay State. He stirred such enthusiasm among the Boston Irish that two regiments were organized for the state, the 28th and 29th Massachusetts. The governor, however, withheld the regiments from the Irish Brigade and appointed natives of the state, none of whom were Irish, as

officers. After Boston, Meagher had similar success in
Philadelphia, sparking the creation of two Pennsylvania
regiments, one infantry, the other cavalry.

Back in New York Tom met with Daniel Devlin and
Judge Charles Daly, two men who had worked hardest
to help him organize the Irish Brigade. The New York
regiments had already gone into training at Fort Schuyler,
on the East River above Manhattan.

"Judge, and you too, Dan," Tom said, "there is no
way to thank you for the cooperation and help you've
given."

"Nonsense, Tom!" the judge exclaimed. "And I speak
for Dan Devlin, as well. We are no less Irish than you, and
no less proud of our people. If you can give so much of
yourself—"

"Perhaps," Tom interrupted, "but nevertheless you
are both busy men. I have only this. But this is not what
I would like to speak of now, for I wish to impose even
more on your time and good services."

"You have only to ask, Tom," Daniel Devlin put in.
"But I think I know what you ask and, speaking for
Judge Daly as well, have no fear. If you wish to join
the regiments and take personal charge at Fort Schuyler,
we will carry on here in New York."

Tom laughed, shaking his head. "Ah, you two are far
too much for me," he said. "Now you read my mind.
True, my place is with the men. But there is one other
thing. I know you have seen to it that equipment and
supplies have been provided. But what of a flag for the
Irish Brigade?"

Judge Daly and Daniel Devlin looked at each other, each grinning widely. Neither answered Meagher's question for a moment. Then the judge spoke.

"You should not have asked, Tom," he said. "We wished to surprise you."

Tom frowned. "You mean a flag has been designed and is ready?"

"Designed, yes. Ready, no," Devlin answered.

"What Dan means," Judge Daly explained, "is that Elizabeth, your good wife, and Mary Barrett, her good friend, have taken upon themselves the sewing of a flag. Wait, wait"—the judge held up his hand—"it will be a flag such as you yourself would have designed. Elizabeth, who knows you from cover to cover, was the inspiration." He went on to describe the standard being prepared for the Irish Brigade, which would be flown side by side with the Stars and Stripes.

Elizabeth Meagher, knowing her husband's devotion to the flag symbolizing the last months of the crushed Irish Rebellion—the gold harp of Tara on a deep green field—had suggested the design. The harp and green field had been retained. A shamrock wreath and sunburst in gold had been added. "And your favorite quote by Ireland's ancient poet, Ossian, will be seen in gold and in Gaelic across the bottom of the banner."

Tom's eyes brightened. "Dear Elizabeth!" he said. "How well she knows me! So the flag will bear the legend *'Never retreat from the clash of spears.'* I could not have asked for better."

"The flag will be ready when the brigade prepares to

leave for Washington," Judge Daly added. "There will
be a ceremony and a blessing outside the residence of the
archbishop on Madison Avenue. His Excellency Archbishop Hughes will present the flag to the brigade."

Thomas Meagher left for Fort Schuyler. There he devoted the next few weeks to supervision of the training
procedures which had been most effectively handled by
his officers, Colonel Nugent and Captains McMahon and
Hogan. Now and then he spoke to the assembled regiments, emphasizing the rightness of the cause for which
they would fight. In what might be considered a melo-
dramatic gesture in anyone else, he would point at the
Stars and Stripes, floating above the gray walls of the
fort, and remind them in the eloquence which had become his trademark that their duty was to keep that
banner flying proudly, and bring it out of every battle
without a spot or stain of dishonor.

On the last Sunday the Irish Brigade would spend at
Fort Schuyler, Irishmen from throughout the New York
area congregated there for the final dress parade. Thomas
Meagher stood on the platform before which the regiments would march, Elizabeth, his senior officers, Judge
Daly, Daniel Devlin and other notables beside him. In
the crowd were the proud wives, children and friends of
the Irish volunteers.

It was a beautiful and exhilarating event. The blue
waters of the East River, just below the fort, sparkled
in the unbroken sunshine of an Indian Summer afternoon, with the white sails of pleasure craft floating along,
and the still green shores of Willet's Point on the op-

posite bank dotted with trim white houses and tall church steeples.

With the sunlight-bathed gray walls of Schuyler as a background, the men of the Irish Brigade marched by, saluting proudly. Colonel Thomas Meagher could hardly contain himself, he was so pleased. Yet, for a fleeting moment his eyes turned sad. If only—and the thought floated in and out of his mind quickly—he'd had such well-trained men beside him in Ireland!

Later that week, on November 18, 1861, Thomas Meagher stood before the same men, assembled now on Madison Avenue, a city block from the fast-rising St. Patrick's Cathedral, to receive the flags of the Irish Brigade from the vicar-general of the Archdiocese of New York. Archbishop Hughes, who was to have made the presentation personally, had been sent by President Lincoln to Europe to keep Catholic countries from recognizing the Confederacy.

Colonel Meagher accepted the flags as acting commander of the Irish Brigade. No word had been received from General Shields. The general had left California before Meagher's invitation to command the brigade arrived on the West Coast, there being at the time no telegraph or telephone, or even a railroad, to connect New York with the Pacific. The officers of the Irish Brigade and the authorities in New York were unanimous in deciding that no one better deserved the command than Thomas Meagher.

The 69th Regiment was the first to leave New York for Washington. Tom, acting chief of the Irish Brigade, led

them out of town, exhilarated as he had not been since
before the fiasco at Kilkenny. Word of the Trent Affair
had just reached New York.

England had been aiding the Confederacy. English-
built ships flying the Confederate flag had been harassing
Union shipping in the Atlantic. The North sent out war
vessels to chase down the Southern privateers and help
blockade the Southern coast.

Jefferson Davis, President of the Confederate States of
America, hoped for recognition of the Confederacy by
Great Britain and other European powers, and sent two
commissioners on a diplomatic mission to Europe. The
two, Senators James Mason and John Slidell, left
Charleston, South Carolina, in secrecy on a blockade run-
ner to Havana, Cuba. There, they sailed for England on
the British steamer *Trent*.

The *Trent* was stopped in the Atlantic by a Union
man-of-war, commanded by Captain Wilkes, exercising
the same "right of search" with which England had been
wont to insult the United States before the War of 1812.
Mason and Slidell were taken prisoners on November 8,
1861.

The English government, already overly friendly to the
Southern cause, castigated the United States for this
insult to the British flag. British troops were rushed to
Canada, and everywhere there was talk of open war between England and America.

For Thomas Meagher this meant war against his lifelong enemy. He was more than ever thrilled at the pros-
pect of fighting for the Union, since that might also mean

fighting against Britain. "War with England is imminent," he said as he was leaving New York. "The Irish Brigade will be the first to meet the music. The regiments remaining here must hold themselves in readiness for their marching orders. Ireland's day has come!"

Those regiments, the 4th and 5th New York, finally left on December 16. On the eighteenth they joined the 69th near Alexandria, Virginia. The following day officers of all three New York regiments met with President Lincoln and urged the appointment of Thomas Meagher as permanent commander of the Irish Brigade. Lincoln, who had great respect for Meagher, sent his name to the Senate for confirmation as brigadier general.

Suddenly, General James Shields appeared in Washington. The offer to command the Irish Brigade had finally reached him in Mexico. When he learned of the situation, Shields sought out President Lincoln, his friend from Illinois days.

"I know that Meagher possesses all the qualities of a good general," he told the President.

The Senate confirmed the appointment of Thomas Meagher as brigadier general on February 5, 1862. The Secretary of War immediately assigned him to full command of the Irish Brigade.

Though he felt a sense of regret, Tom was gratified by the honor. He had never considered the possibility of personally commanding the Irish Brigade. He had organized it with the sincere intention that it be headed by General Shields. He had been determined to accept no other responsibility but that of an aide on Shields's staff.

He yielded and accepted the command only after the officers of the brigade insisted.

The Irish Brigade was first ordered to Warrenton Junction, west of Washington, a mud-mired, marshy area of Virginia, to operate with the Army of the Potomac commanded by Major General George B. McClellan. McClellan had enjoyed some success in western Virginia, though those closest to the action credited his second-in-command, Brigadier General William S. Rosecrans, for the strategies that brought victory. There were at least 150,000 men under McClellan. His matériel of war included two hundred pieces of artillery.

Meagher waited for orders to join McClellan. They did not come. He and his men became impatient as they heard reports from Washington urging McClellan to move to Richmond. Months passed with no activity. Finally President Lincoln, disturbed by McClellan's seeming stubbornness, ordered him to advance. On March 15, 1862, Meagher received his orders from McClellan. "The time for action has arrived," McClellan had written.

"It's about time," one of the men of the 69th was heard to mutter, as the Irish Brigade was notified that all should be ready to march the next morning.

With the 69th Regiment leading, the Irish Brigade started for Fairfax Court House. They were to be attached to the corps commanded by Brigadier General Sumner. As part of McClellan's Army of the Potomac, they were to intercept General Joseph Johnston, the Confederate hero of Bull Run, drive him back from Richmond and occupy the rebel capital.

Meagher fully expected that they would march straight south in Virginia to meet Johnston, who was guarding Richmond. It was the fastest, most practical course to take. McClellan, following his seemingly regular strategy of taking his time and delaying action as long as possible, had other ideas. He decided that his entire army would board ships on the Potomac, travel down through Chesapeake Bay to Fort Monroe at the tip of the peninsula formed by the juncture of the York and James Rivers. He would then march the army northward up the peninsula and approach Richmond from the south.

The army landed at Fort Monroe without incident and started north, beginning what was called the Peninsula Campaign. The army did not continue toward Richmond without a break. McClellan suddenly decided to attack Yorktown. A full month was wasted besieging the city before the Confederates withdrew to Williamsburg. McClellan did not follow, but ordered the advance toward Richmond. Sumner's Corps and the Irish Brigade made camp less than twenty miles from the Confederate capital, on the east bank of the Chickahominy River. McClellan and the balance of the army went five miles further, traveling the west bank of the river.

Again the Irish Brigade was subjected to inactivity. Day followed day with no orders. Two weeks passed. Then, the evening of Saturday, May 31, the night air was suddenly filled with the thunder of cannon. No other responsibility but that of an aide on Shields' staff. from not far away along the Chickahominy as the battle of Seven Pines raged on. Confederate forces under Hill, Huger, Smith and Longstreet were being attacked by

General Casey's Federal troops near the Williamsburg
road. They had fought on through a torrential rainstorm
the night of May 30.

The evening of May 31, after two weeks of waiting,
Meagher was watching steeplechase races organized by
his men to relieve their boredom. Suddenly the night air,
already echoing with occasional rifle fire, was blasted by
the roar of cannon nearby. Tom stood up, keenly listening to the thunder of artillery and the crackle of musket
fire. McClellan, he thought, had been caught by Joe
Johnston with the Federals split by the flooding Chickahominy. Johnston, an able soldier and tactician, would
pour all his might against McClellan, hoping to crush
him before reinforcements could cross the raging river.

A courier rode up on horseback with orders for Sumner's Corps, including the Irish Brigade, to get into the
battle. In less than thirty minutes the brigade was on the
move. The night was black. Not a star was visible overhead. The river had become so swollen that the lone
bridge crossing the Chickahominy had been washed out.
Men had to wade across with water up to their chests and
necks. The artillery had to be abandoned on the shore.

Action had halted for the night. As Meagher led his
regiment toward a withered oak tree that was to be their
headquarters, and around which the men would deploy
themselves for some sleep, his heart sank. Here and there
he had to step over a body clotted and starched with
blood or a dead horse. Under the whitened oak he finally
stretched himself out and closed his eyes.

Tom Meagher and the Irish Brigade woke the following morning to a bright sun filtering through the dense trees. As they looked about, their eyes, widening in surprise, met others exhibiting as much astonishment. They had bivouacked within a pistol-shot range of a Confederate regiment. They had come two miles from the flooded Chickahominy. Richmond was only four miles ahead.

The battle of Fair Oaks resumed, with the Irish Brigade aiming to drive the enemy back behind the Pamunkey and Richmond railroad some five hundred yards away. The Confederates, on the other hand, were determined to drive the Federals back to the Chickahominy and into its tumbling waters if possible.

A Federal force succeeded in crossing the railroad and blazed away at a regiment of Georgia volunteers. The rebels continued retreating into a dense forest beyond the tracks, tearing their way through swamp and underbrush.

"Now, men!" Meagher called to his 69th.

He led them in a quick sweep to the railroad. Under a rain of bullets the Irish deployed into a line of battle along the tracks. An enemy force had swung along their flank as they deployed and gunfire was exchanged for over an hour. Finally the Confederate troops retreated.

"Well done, men!" Meagher exulted. "The chivalry of Virginia has met its match in the chivalry of Tipperary!"

With Meagher leading, the men of the New York 69th advanced into the woods after the retreating Confederates. And so it was throughout the sector. The rebels were pushed back on the right by Major General John Sedgwick. Brigadier General Richardson pushed through the middle. Major General Kearney hit hard on the left flank.

The enemy was in full retreat. General Joe Johnston had been wounded, though his troops did not know it at the time, and the remnants of his army tore through the choking dust of the roads under a blistering sun for the possible safety of Richmond's streets.

Generals Meagher, Kearney, Sedgwick and Richardson were ready to follow Brigadier General "Fighting Joe" Hooker into the Confederate capital.

"Now that we've got 'em on the run," one soldier called out, "the thing's to keep 'em running!"

Meagher and the other generals were equally sure that Richmond would fall if they could continue the assault. General McClellan, supreme in command, decided against it. He ordered the left wing of his army to entrench itself four miles from Richmond. As part of that wing, General Meagher deployed the Irish Brigade as he was ordered.

McClellan's mistake, if indeed it was a mistake, might have cost the Union a quick end to the war and victory. With General Joseph Johnston badly wounded, Lieutenant General Robert E. Lee, considered one of history's great military geniuses, took over command of the Confederate army with Stonewall Jackson as his chief lieutenant. Lee and Jackson began a series of attacks on McClellan, broke his line of supplies and kept him on the defensive.

Meagher, perhaps the most disappointed of the many generals who regretted McClellan's indecisiveness, had little time to worry about what might have been. McClellan had decided on a gradual retreat of the main army as Lee's forces kept pushing toward him. Friday morning, June 27, McClellan ordered Brigadier General McCall, in charge of a force of thirty thousand men and sixty pieces of cannon, to fall back on the bridges crossing the Chickahominy at Gaines Mill and make a stand against the enemy as a cover for his retreat. Lee was advancing toward the Union lines with a force of nearly eighty thousand and sixty cannon.

Just before noon the battle began with the roar of 120 cannon tearing through the countryside. So thick was the smoke that it shut out the light of the bright summer day and dimmed the gleam of bayonet and flash of musket. The Confederates made charge after charge, almost reckless in their fury. The Federal infantry met them head-on, held on stubbornly, repulsing charge after charge. Outnumbered, the Federals were becoming exhausted. They were also running low on ammunition. It was obvious that reinforcements were badly needed, or else the superior numbers of the enemy would sweep through their lines.

At this point orders were sent to Fair Oaks, where the Irish Brigade was still encamped. Meagher and his fighting Irish, along with a second brigade, were sent, double quick, across the five miles that separated them from the battlefield. They arrived to find the Federal troops retreating stubbornly.

With Meagher leading the Irish Brigade and Brigadier General French the second brigade of reinforcements, the fresh soldiers pushed their way through the retreating masses and gained the crest of a hill. Meagher's blood surged hotly through his veins. This was the kind of action he relished.

He and General French gave the order to charge simultaneously. With a wild shout, which was echoed by his men, Meagher led his brigade of Irish volunteers down the hill toward the enemy. Anticipating a quick victory, the rebel force had not expected the charge.

Through a hail of shot and bullets Meagher's men drove on, coming face to face with their adversaries. Furious and reckless as they had been, the Confederates were unprepared for the daredevil, fire-eating bravado of the Irish. The infantry and artillery of the Confederates fell back after a fierce but brief struggle. This gave time for the Federals who had been in retreat to regroup themselves behind the brigades of Generals Meagher and French. The Union army, until a few moments before in danger of capture or annihilation, moved across the Chickahominy in safety. Meagher and his brigade were the last to cross the river.

It had been a gallant rescue. Meagher, astride his horse on the east bank, looked down affectionately at the panting, happy men of his brigade, standing as they were between the soldiers they had helped save and those they had defeated.

X

THE INJUSTICE
OF THE JUST

The thrilling charge of the Irish Brigade, which had
helped rescue McClellan's army, took place on the third
day of what came to be known as the Seven Days' Battle
around Richmond. These seven days spanned the period
June 25 to July 1, 1862. With the army's safety at least
temporarily assured, the two brigades which had saved
the day were withdrawn. Meagher's Irish rejoined General Sumner's Corps at Fair Oaks, June 27.

Two days later, on June 29, General Sumner broke
camp at Fair Oaks, moving to Allen's Farm, between
Orchard and Savage stations. There the enemy struck
furiously at the right flank of General Sedgwick's division but were driven back. The following day, hearing
that the Confederates had crossed the Chickahominy and
were moving toward Savage's Station, General Sumner
moved his corps forward, deploying them in an open field
to the left of the railroad. At four o'clock on the afternoon of a blistering hot day, the two sides clashed. With

one regiment of the Irish Brigade making another furious charge during the six hours of battle, the enemy was driven off and the retreat of the Federals continued.

The Confederate brigades were regrouped and renewed their pursuit of the backward-moving Army of the Potomac. Catching up with the Federals at White Oak Swamp, Lee's army began a vigorous shelling of two divisions of McClellan's forces, pushing them ever rearward. General Sumner again called on Meagher.

"Take your boys," he said, "and go in and save another day."

Meagher and the Irish Brigade rushed into action, meeting the enemy at Glendale, not far from Charles City, between the Chickahominy and James Rivers. It was a bloody battle, furiously fought, with three Union generals wounded and hundreds of men killed. The Irish Brigade again helped save the day. Despite the losses, when the battle ended in the dead of night, the enemy had been routed and driven off. But there was no rest for the Irish Brigade.

The next day the Confederates assaulted the Federal lines again, this time at Malvern Hill. Three times the Irish Brigade was called upon to charge the enemy. Each time General Thomas Meagher, the green plume in his hat dancing in the breeze and his sword flashing under the bright sun, led his men through a storm of bullets.

Ordered back for the third time the brigade was sent in at the last moment. It was the wildest, most reckless charge of all, with the green plume still leading the way. Suddenly the plume disappeared. Thomas Meagher's head had bobbed down momentarily. A rifle ball had passed through the rim of his hat within a quarter inch of his right temple. As quickly as the plume had disappeared, it reappeared. The charge continued even more viciously. They accomplished their mission, saving the left wing of the Federal army from being turned. Again the Irish Brigade of Thomas Meagher had saved a possible disaster.

It was a dearly bought victory for the Irish Brigade. Though Thomas Meagher had been miraculously saved, there was a heavy loss in men and officers. Lieutenant Reynolds of the 69th was killed. Captains Leddy and O'Donovan and Lieutenant Cahill were severely wounded.

It was the greatest blow the brigade had suffered up to that time. Meagher, concerned that his brigade might be wiped out, wrote the Secretary of War. When the Irish Brigade was formed, he had been promised continuing recruitment for his regiments. He had heard nothing as yet.

The battle of Malvern Hill was the last in the Seven Days' Battle and ended the Peninsula Campaign of General McClellan. His Army of the Potomac had reached the safety of Harrison's Landing and the general could consider a change in his strategy of taking Richmond. He was not to have the chance. Lincoln replaced McClellan with Major General John Pope.

Pope immediately ordered a total withdrawal of all Federal troops from the peninsula. The day the Irish Brigade was scheduled to leave, General Meagher discussed the condition of his regiments with his most trusted aide, Lieutenant Temple Emmett.

"We might engage in another battle, perhaps two," Emmett told him. "All the regiments have lost so many men, any further losses would cripple their efficiency in battle."

"I've written the Secretary of War, Mr. Stanton, reminding him of the War Department's promise to fill our ranks when needed."

"Can you wait, Tom?" Emmett asked. "Remember, Simon Cameron and not Edwin Stanton was Secretary of War when the Irish Brigade was authorized. It may take him some time to make up his mind what to do."

Tom nodded. "Perhaps you're right," he said. A thought flashed through his mind. "Perhaps a trip to New York might help fill our regiments. I'm sure General Sumner will grant us both leave if I explain the situation."

"Us both?" Emmett asked.

"Yes, both," Tom replied. "I want you with me."

Sumner, depending greatly on the Irish Brigade which had distinguished itself so admirably, immediately agreed. Thomas Meagher, accompanied by Lieutenant Temple Emmett, arrived in New York filled with hope. He had had such great success in recruiting when the Irish Brigade was first activated that he anticipated no trouble.

He made several stirring speeches, the last of them at the armory of New York's famed 7th Regiment. But while his reception was always warm, he had little success. Others had been ahead of him in recruiting, and several new regiments were already being raised in the city. Insidious rumors hurt his recruitment efforts even more.

Newspaper reports of the Irish Brigade's action in Virginia had been overheavy with praise of General Thomas Meagher. When these stories appeared side-by-side with the long lists of the dead and wounded, tongues began to wag.

"The papers tell us Meagher led the charge," someone would say. "But if he was in front, how is it so many behind him were killed and he not scratched?"

Young men would hear this. And they would see a friend return home with only one leg or read the name of a chum who would never come back. As a result they would think twice before enlisting, however persuasive General Thomas Meagher might be.

"It would be suicide to join the Irish Brigade," they said.

It hardly mattered that the papers supported Meagher, that they made it clear he had taken even greater chances than his men, that he was still alive only by the grace of God and an inch in a bullet's trajectory. Recruits still held back.

Those who respected and admired Meagher did all they could. Members of the New York Corn Exchange raised a fund by personal subscription to pay a bounty to the first three hundred who would enlist in the Irish Brigade. Austin Kelly and Company equaled the Corn Exchange bounty for the first fifty volunteers and added unbroken employment for the duration of the war to their wives and daughters.

Nothing helped. Enlistments for the Irish Brigade were few.

Thomas Meagher, hurt and discouraged, felt helpless. But he knew there was still a war to be won. He and Temple Emmett returned to Virginia to find the Union had suffered even more critical losses.

General Robert E. Lee had sent Stonewall Jackson against General Pope's army. Jackson had pushed the Union forces back to the Rappahannock River. Pope prematurely attacked the Confederates. General James Longstreet made a counterattack and drove the Federals back across Bull Run. The Union suffered its second defeat at Bull Run and Lee's strategy was successful. He pushed further toward Washington, capturing the arsenal at Harper's Ferry with its eleven thousand defenders, and crossed the Potomac into Maryland. The Confederates had finally set foot on Union territory.

At this point General Pope was replaced. General George B. McClellan was restored to command of the Army of the Potomac. He immediately started after Lee, now entrenched in Maryland and planning to encircle Washington and attack it from the east. McClellan advanced toward Frederick with nearly ninety thousand men.

The moment he arrived back in Virginia, General Meagher was given orders to have the Irish Brigade board ships at Fort Monroe and to proceed to the Washington

area to join forces with McClellan's army. Though the
regiments had been weakened seriously through loss of
manpower, the men cheered their return to action.

September 16, 1862, found the Confederate army
ranged along a ridge near Sharpsburg, Maryland, on the
west side of Antietam Creek. General Hooker, with
seventeen thousand men, crossed the creek in the dead
of night, maneuvering from the extreme right of the
Confederate line. He charged Lee's left and center in a
battle that raged through the following afternoon.

The enemy position was exceptionally strong, fortified
by a huge force of infantry and cavalry and numerous
batteries of artillery. Hooker's men had driven the enemy
from the ridge into open fields and from there into a
dense woods. But Hooker, along with five other Union
generals, was wounded. With General Sumner's Corps
assigned to replace Hooker's tiring troops, the Irish Brigade swept into action.

Again General Meagher led them in an advance under
heavy fire. They mounted the crest of a hill, beyond
which the Confederates were solidly entrenched in a
sunken road and throughout a cornfield. The Irish Brigade unleashed a relentless firing into the ditch and cornfield, following with a charge down the hill.

Suddenly Meagher's body went catapulting from his
horse. The animal had been shot from under him. Un-
hurt, he grabbed the reins of a horse running loose and
remounted. General Sumner saw Meagher's fall and
wasted not a moment sending a force under Brigadier

General Caldwell to relieve the Irish Brigade. The exchange was made as evenly and steadily as might have been accomplished on the drill field.

The battle of Antietam raged for fourteen hours with nearly 200,000 men and five hundred pieces of artillery taking part. It was the bloodiest single day of fighting so far in the war, and ended as night shrouded the battlefield. Entire regiments had been mowed down, in a stand that was as heroic for one side as for the other. The action stopped with neither army beaten, but with both too exhausted to go on.

Lee, having lost over one fourth of his army, withdrew back across the Potomac into Virginia with hardly forty thousand men. Lincoln urged McClellan, who still commanded 100,000, not to allow Lee to escape. The overcautious McClellan hesitated. When Lincoln finally lost patience, he again removed McClellan from command, appointing Major General Ambrose Burnside in his stead.

After the battle of Antietam, Thomas Meagher was thoroughly dismayed by the extent of the losses suffered by the Irish Brigade. He had taken 317 men of the 69th Regiment into the assault, 196 of whom had been killed or wounded. The complete Irish Brigade had 540 casualties. How could they, he wondered, participate in even one more skirmish!

Help came unexpectedly in November, and Meagher felt a resurgence of hope. The 116th Pennsylvania Regiment, a group of all-Irish volunteers, was attached to the Irish Brigade. And soon after, the 28th Massachusetts, which Governor Andrew had summarily taken away from Meagher though it had been specifically organized for him, was transferred from its earlier assignment. Even so, the entire Irish Brigade now numbered no more than 1,300 men.

"It's a help," Tom said to Temple Emmett, "even though the whole brigade numbers hardly more than the sixty-ninth did alone when first we started."

Now General Burnside was ready for action. Unfortunately he was as rash as McClellan had been cautious. Rather than move against Lee with a hope of crushing his army, Burnside—whose army numbered some 120,000—decided to capture Richmond. He deployed his force, including the Irish Brigade, north of the Rappahannock River near Fredericksburg, Virginia. From that location, sixty miles south of Washington and just fifty-three miles north of Richmond, he would march on the Confederate capital.

Burnside had not considered the natural impregnability of Fredericksburg, easy to defend and most difficult to attack. At that point, both sides of the Rappahannock are hilly. The hills on the north bank where Burnside positioned his army were parallel with the water with little space between the base of the hills and the river.

General Lee's position on the south side was the opposite. There the hills swung in a half circle about six miles long and over two miles wide, forming a plain within which Fredericksburg lay. Behind the city the hills rise high and barren. To the east they are low and dense with trees. To counter any move of Burnside's, Lee

set 85,000 men and three hundred cannon to the south
bank and destroyed every bridge to the north or south
of the town. He posted General Longstreet and his rugged
corps on Marye's Hill.

Thomas Meagher stood with Temple Emmett on one
side of the hills across the Rappahannock. He looked
down the steep incline to the water, then across at the
spread of Lee's troops. He shook his head in bewilder-
ment.

"I don't know, Emmett," he muttered, half to himself.
"How we can attack so strong a position I cannot imagine."

Emmett pointed toward Marye's Hill. "Our scouts report there is a large stone wall behind the road fronting
Marye's Hill," he said. "Riflemen back of that wall can
pick off our men one by one."

With other commanders, General Meagher protested
the attack on Lee's position at Fredericksburg. Burnside
insisted on going ahead with his plan. Early the morning
of December 11 he had engineers placing pontoons in
the waters of the Rappahannock. They were to form five
bridges over which Burnside would lead the Union army.

The next day Burnside started his men across. Before
evening most of his troops were on the south side of the
Rappahannock and occupying the city of Fredericksburg.
They had experienced no difficulty up to that point and
Burnside was elated. On December 13 Burnside ordered
the troops to line up in attacking columns. He was ready
to begin his assault on Lee's fortifications outside the
town.

Meagher, his men in formation before him, walked past each of the four regiments in the Irish Brigade, speaking a few words to each. He returned to the head of the first column and led them out for the attack. Marye's Hill was the target of the Irish Brigade.

As the columns neared the hill, Longstreet's forces opened fire. Ranks broke. Drums rolled and bugles sounded. Broken ranks closed and the brigade resumed its march.

The stone wall came into sight. As they neared it, heads—and hands wielding muskets and rifles—poked themselves above the wall and rained fire on the Irish. Meagher led five charges against the stone wall without effect. Each charge was made over friends and comrades who were wounded, dying or dead.

General Lee, watching the impossible thrusts, turned to one of his aides. "Never were men so brave," he said of Meagher and his Irish Brigade. "They ennoble their race by their gallantry."

The hopeless thrusts were finally stopped by the dark of night. Burnside finally gave up and ordered a retreat. Over 2,500 men were lost in the ill-conceived attack on Fredericksburg, 541 members of the Irish Brigade, which now numbered a mere 874 men.

The Union army had retrated into the city of Fredericksburg. In the safety of the town Burnside called his officers into council. Still determined to defeat Lee, however much it cost, he laid plans for renewing the attack the following day.

Almost every one of his generals protested. Burnside

remained adamant. The generals argued until they might have been court-martialed for gross insubordination. Finally, when Burnside's most respected aides backed the dissenting generals, he relented.

One of Meagher's closest friends, William Horgan, had been killed in the battle. When his body was not found among those being readied for burial in Fredericksburg, Tom had the burial squads make a special search. They discovered the body not far from the disastrous stone wall. Tom had the body embalmed and accompanied it back to New York. He arrived there at noon Christmas Day.

At the funeral for Major William Horgan, Tom Meagher was taken sick, remaining in bed for two weeks. By the time he was able to return to duty, his Irish Brigade was in winter quarters at Falmouth, not far from Fredericksburg.

Meagher had expected to find an answer to his letter addressed to Secretary of War Edwin Stanton. There was none. Tom, thoroughly perplexed by the seeming indifference of the War Department, ached inside. He was torn between his duty as a soldier, his love for America and what it stood for and his responsibility to the Irish Brigade as its commander. Weakened as it was, stripped to a ludicrously low complement of men, how could he, in conscience, send it back into battle?

"I cannot understand it," he told his aide, Temple Emmett. "McClellan, and other generals we have served under—all except Burnside—have praised the brigade for its bravery. All have reported that again and again our men have saved the day. Yet we get no help, especially now when it is so badly needed."

"It's no secret," Emmett reminded Tom, "that Burnside resented the disagreement of his officers with his plan for Fredericksburg. He has been especially bitter about you. Did you know he even asked the President to have General Hooker court-martialed for insubordination?"

Tom nodded. "Nothing will come of it," he said. "Hooker is too fine a soldier and Lincoln knows that. Emmett, exactly how many of our men are fit for battle?"

"This morning only five hundred and twenty-one of the eight hundred and seventy-four remaining in the brigade could answer a roll call," Emmett replied.

Tom shook his head dejectedly. "Even should the other three hundred and fifty-three recover before the fighting is resumed, the brigade would be helpless," he moaned. "Another Fredericksburg would wipe us out." He hesitated, then continued: "What I cannot understand is that before Fredericksburg both the President and the Secretary of War said that the Irish Brigade should be strengthened while we were laid up in winter quarters."

"Remember," Emmett said. "That was before Fredericksburg. Before Burnside."

"I must still believe the War Department will do something for us," Tom said. "I'm going to write again to Secretary Stanton."

That very day, February 20, 1863, Thomas Meagher sent another request for help to the Secretary of War. It was a long letter, outlining the many accomplishments of the Irish Brigade and its tremendous losses. He pointed out the condition of the war and its possible lengthy duration, emphasizing that he was not asking for any special consideration, only that which had been given already to other commands.

For whatever reason, no answer came from Secretary Stanton. He did not acknowledge receipt of the request.

Soon after Meagher's letter was sent to Stanton, Lincoln—as if in reply to Burnside's demand for a court-martial of General Joseph Hooker—replaced Burnside with Hooker as commander of the Army of the Potomac.

Next to the end of the war or the granting of his request for added manpower in the Irish Brigade, this was the best possible news for Tom Meagher.

"We may not get more men in time," he told Emmett, "but General Hooker is a fine soldier and a fair man. We can fight till our blood runs for such a man."

It was now March. Soon it would be St. Patrick's Day, and no day is of greater significance to the Irish. Tom called on Temple Emmett.

"Lieutenant Emmett," he said with a grin, "March seventeenth will soon be upon us."

Emmett's own grin was ear-to-ear. "Sure and begorra!" he joked. "And did the general think I needed reminding?"

Tom laughed. "Perhaps not. But our men need a lifting of their spirits. How better than with a celebration on the great day? Put the men to work building a chapel. We can begin the holy saint's feast day with Mass in a proper setting for Father Corby."

The chapel was built, a huge affair constructed mainly of poles and tent canvas. As would be expected, it was lavishly decorated with green inside and out. With no paint available, the men of the Irish Brigade cut branches and sprigs from evergreen trees, bunching them into wreaths and braiding them into many shapes.

A large reviewing stand was also built, this in front of the general headquarters and facing an extensive open area where games and reviews would be staged. Meagher sent invitations in the name of the brigade to all officers attached to the Army of the Potomac. His men told others in all regiments at Falmouth that they were welcome.

By the time March 17 dawned, nature had also done its best to further the beauty and pleasure of the day. An early Maryland spring brought a lush green to trees, bushes and grass. Everywhere one turned it was *Erin go brath!*

Green was not the only color to brighten the balmy, sun-drenched day. The varied uniforms worn by the regiments of the Army of the Potomac provided many contrasts. There were, of course, blouses and trousers in many shades of blue, including the regulation deep-blue. And there were a few from the 79th New York in tartan kilts, Garibaldi Guards in broad-brimmed, plumed hats and New York Fire Zouaves in billowing red or white trousers and multihued embroidered jackets and tasseled caps.

General Hooker and his staff arrived early enough so that the general attended the St. Patrick's Day Mass in the makeshift tent-chapel. He then went out to the reviewing stand to join the other generals of the army. General Thomas Meagher had preceded him by just a few minutes, appropriately dressed for the occasion with green the predominant color. He also wore a rosette formed of blue ribbon on his coat, blue having been the national color of ancient Ireland.

As soon as General Hooker arrived on the reviewing stand, a loud cheer went up from the hundreds of soldiers massed about the platform. The general went immediately to Meagher and, with an arm about Tom's shoulder, drew him to the center of the platform. He raised his other hand for silence.

"Today," he called out in a loud voice, "the cheers belong only to this man, General Thomas Francis Meagher, and his Irish Brigade. And I say 'God bless the Irish Brigade!'"

A riotous cheer split the air at his words. The rest of the day was given over to games and general pleasure.

The following weeks were quiet. The Army of the Potomac remained in its winter quarters in Maryland. During the last week of March, Thomas Meagher was given leave to visit New York and help in a relief campaign for Ireland. The green isle, the home he would never forget, was again suffering famine. Meagher, Archbishop Hughes of New York, Horace Greeley, the founder and editor of the New York *Tribune*, and General George B. McClellan were to be the speakers at a meeting at the Academy of Music.

Meagher gave one of his typical heart-warming speeches, pleading for help for "an Ireland, bowed down though she be, steeped in gall, and gnawed with misery to the bone." His speech, and those of the other celebrities, helped open the hearts and pocketbooks of New Yorkers. Thousands of dollars were collected that night to help the unfortunate of Ireland.

Thomas Meagher returned to Maryland and his Irish Brigade on April 26. He was immediately ordered to report to Major General Winfield Scott Hancock, under whose command the Irish Brigade would operate as part of General Hooker's Army of the Potomac. General Hancock greeted him enthusiastically.

"We are most fortunate to have such a leader in our command," Hancock told him. "I sympathize with the reduced strength of your Irish Brigade and shall do what I can to help."

"You can count on me and my men for whatever help we can give," Meagher said. "As long as one of us remains to fight, we will."

"I know that, General," Hancock assured Meagher. "Your record speaks for itself. I've already ordered your brigade along the Rappahannock west of Fredericksburg. General Hooker's plan is to advance on Chancellorsville. We need your brigade's gallantry in that sector."

Meagher found the Irish Brigade encamped near one of the fords crossing the Rappahannock. General Hooker's army was already under way. Thirty-six thousand of his men had been ordered to cross the river and swing quietly around the left of Lee's Confederates near Chancellorsville. Once there, situated between Richmond and Lee's protective force, they were to entrench and wait.

The Irish Brigade was to form the extreme right of Hooker's advance force.

The night of April 30, General Thomas Meagher led the Irish Brigade across the Rappahannock under a bright moon. The regiments camped on the southern bank of the river, guarding a crossing near the principal road from Chancellorsville to Richmond. The march was resumed the next morning. Before midnight they arrived at Scott's Mill, the position they were to defend. Meagher called his staff officers for a conference. He held a lantern over a map of the area.

"This is our position at Scott's Mill," he said, pointing to the map. He moved his finger left. "Here is Chancellorsville, perhaps two miles away. And this road," he added, indicating a line moving south, "leads from the town directly to the left wing of Lee's army. The reason why we must hold this point is obvious, since it gives us control of a sector between Lee and Richmond."

He gave quick orders for deploying guns and stationing riflemen and pickets. His men guarded the position throughout the night. At eight the next morning, they began to hear the rattle of heavy fire from the vicinity of Chancellorsville. A hard battle was certainly under way.

It was. General Hooker had been outthought by Robert E. Lee. Hooker had felt certain that, when Lee discovered the Army of the Potomac had taken the offensive, he would rush his troops back toward Richmond. But Lee was a matchless tactician, far superior to Hooker. He had been advised by his scouts that Hooker had divided his army, a serious mistake under the circumstances. Instead of retreating toward Richmond, Lee assigned General Stonewall Jackson to attack that part of the Union forces which Hooker had brought to Chancellorsville. With this strategy Lee was doing what Hooker had done, divide his army, but in his case it was a brilliant move.

Hooker's surprise was complete. Jackson, with 25,000 men in gray, swung behind his entrenchments and attacked from the rear. He had been able to do so because of dense woods behind the deployed Federals. As the battle raged furiously, Jackson drove the Union army back into its entrenchments, but though he made a number of assaults, he was unable to capture the positions.

Panic, however, struck at one sector. The Eleventh Army Corps, guarding the Gordonsville Road, was hit so hard on its flank that the men were sure the entire Confederate Army was swarming in on them. They turned and ran, through road and woods, reaching the position held by the Irish Brigade, Scott's Mill.

Meagher stopped their rush by throwing a contingent of soldiers across their path. When he heard their story, he persuaded them to rejoin their comrades. His gifted tongue probably saved panic from spreading throughout Hooker's army.

The battle continued throughout the day and into the night. Though Lee's forces held the Federals in check, the Confederates suffered a great loss. In the dusk of evening, General Stonewall Jackson was mistaken for an enemy officer and shot by one of his own men.

Meagher received orders to lead the Irish Brigade into the fight the next morning, Sunday, May 3. Their assignment was to lend support to the 5th Maine, ranged outside a wooded area overlooking Chancellorsville. The Irish Brigade trudged for three hours, sloshing through swamps and woods. They joined the 5th Maine under a blanket of relentless gunfire. Meagher, riding at the front of the column, had bullets miss him by inches several times.

Though it was deployed in a position exposed to enemy fire, the 5th Maine supported by the Irish Brigade fought valiantly for two hours, holding their ground until all the horses and men of the Maine volunteers were killed or wounded. Near the end of the second hour, a corporal and a private of the 5th Maine, discovering they could no longer operate their guns, blew up the caissons.

Meagher, seeing what was happening, rushed men of his brigade to save the guns. They succeeded in stopping the corporal and private from further destroying the cannon. They then seized the ropes and, under a terrible enemy fusillade, pulled the guns into the woods. Several of Meagher's men were killed while tugging at the ropes, but as soon as one fell another took his place. They worked without a stop until the entire battery was out of danger.

"Fine work, men," General Meagher told them when the job was accomplished. "May God rest those who were killed, but it had to be done. If the enemy had captured those guns, they would have been turned on us. And who knows what the end might have been!"

At that moment General Hancock rode up and called to Meagher.

"General Meagher!" Hancock shouted. "You command the retreat!"

General Hooker had finally given up. Lee's army, though it had lost a great commander in Stonewall Jackson, had been reunited. Hooker's was still divided. Hooker had decided to retreat and evacuate the strong positions the Federals had held between Chancellorsville and Richmond. The Union army crossed to the other side of the Rappahannock on Wednesday, May 6, returning to their old camp at Fredericksburg. The Irish Brigade now had fifty men fewer than before the battle of Chancellorsville.

Twice General Robert E. Lee had beaten back the best the Federals had to offer. Twice the Union forces had been within the shadow of Richmond, and twice they had been forced to retreat. The only bright spot in the whole debacle had been the gallantry of the Irish Brigade.

General Thomas Meagher, resting at Fredericksburg, pondered the events of the previous few months. He had not as yet received either an answer or acknowledgment of his request for additional men. He was uncertain as to his next move.

Meagher knew that a strong public feeling against the war was beginning to manifest itself in many parts of the North. It was a tragic thing, he thought. And even more tragic was the vilification of Lincoln. Even Northerners were calling the President a tyrant and a murderer, and referring to the war itself as a wicked murder.

Just a few months before, on January 1, 1863, Lincoln had taken a step that changed the whole aspect of the war, raised it to a higher, more noble plane. He had issued his Emancipation Proclamation. With it had gone any fear of foreign nations recognizing the Confederacy. For, since

Russia had freed its serfs in 1861, the South was almost alone in the world in adhering to the practise of slavery.

The North had been stopped again and again on the battlefield. Could it still win? General Thomas Meagher was still convinced that it could. He was not sure, however, what part—if any—he might play in the victory that had to come.

Tom wondered if it would be possible to remain—and he fervently wished he could—commanding his brigade, crippled as it was. He was needed. Every solitary man was needed.

When he had first heard of the Emancipation Proclamation, his already unshakable respect for President Lincoln increased tremendously. It had been a courageous step, Tom thought, especially with the Union suffering such losses, and he had convinced himself that the action would bring immediate success against the rebels. But it had not. To the contrary, those early months of 1863 were the gloomiest and most tragic of the war, as much off, as on, the battlefield.

There had been violent repercussions to Lincoln's action. In the North the "antis" had gathered strength, accusing the government of exceeding its Constitutional authority. And the South, as could be expected, was even more outraged. They had protested strongly against the North's use of Negro troops, raising an outcry identical with that of the colonists against Indians being employed in battle. Southerners had actually threatened to hang any Federal officer who commanded black soldiers.

The situation also had a negative effect on recruitment. In the spring, when Lincoln again called for volunteers, few responded. So it became necessary to resort to conscription, placing the names of all able-bodied men in a box and drawing out the required number. Those whose names were drawn were compelled to serve in the army or buy substitutes.

Appalled and grieved by what was happening, Tom was on the horns of a dilemma. Three months had passed since he had sent his letter to the Secretary of War and had not had the courtesy of an acknowledgment. The army, he knew, needed the help of every available man. Yet, how in conscience could he take his Irish Brigade again into battle. Diminished in numbers as it was, it could hardly be an effective fighting force. He would be needlessly sacrificing brave men, sending them to certain death. He agonized for hours over his decision. Finally, on May 8, he tendered his resignation as commander of the remnant of a brigade which remained, addressing it to his immediate superior, Major General W. S. Hancock.

His long letter of resignation outlined not only the accomplishments of his men, of which he was proud, but also his disappointment at not receiving an acknowledgment of his letter to the Secretary of War. He then went on to say:

"It would be my greatest happiness, as it would surely be my highest honor, to remain in the companionship and charge of my men; but to do so any longer would be to perpetrate a public deception, in which the hard-won honors of good soldiers, and in them the military reputation of a brave old race, would inevitably be involved and compromised. I cannot be a party to this wrong. My heart, my conscience, my pride, all that is truthful, manful, sincere and just within me forbid it.

In tendering my resignation, however, as the brigadier general in command of this poor vestige and relic of the Irish Brigade, I beg sincerely to assure you that my services, in any capacity that can prove useful, are freely at the summons and disposition of the Government of the United States. That government, and the cause, and the liberty, the noble memories and the future it represents, are entitled, unquestionably and unequivocally, to the life of every citizen who has sworn allegiance to it, and partaken of its grand protection. But while I offer my own life to sustain this good government, I feel it to be my first duty to do nothing that will wantonly imperil the lives of others. . . ."

General Hancock forwarded the resignation to Secretary of War Stanton. He wasted no time in accepting the resignation. On May 14 Thomas Meagher received the official notification. That same evening the Irish Brigade massed into formation to say good-bye to its commander.

It was a sorrowful parting for both Meagher and his men. Meagher thanked them in a choked voice and bade them good luck. Then, one by one, his officers came to him and shook his hand. Finally, Meagher passed by each of the men, shaking each hand with a "Good-bye, and may God bless you." The morning of May 15, Thomas Meagher returned to New York.

The Irish Brigade was no more. The Fighting Irish, as they were now being called, had become a legend.

XI

"FIGHTING SOLDIERS IS ONE THING..."

The high regard and affection of the men of the Irish Brigade for Thomas Meagher was matched by the city of New York. When Tom arrived home in late May 1863, he was welcomed in typical New York fashion as a returning hero. There were parades, banquets and other testimonials. For Tom, however, they seemed empty honors.

Though he had been badly treated by the War Department, he could not erase from his heart and mind the feeling that he was needed, that he was shirking a sacred duty.

"It is only the sight of you that makes all this bearable," he told his wife Elizabeth. "At night I dream always that I again lead my brigade through mists of morning, and I hear the call of trumpets and the rattle of gunfire."

"I thought as much, my darling," Elizabeth said. "The way you toss and turn in your sleep, one would think you were advancing on the enemy. Perhaps you should go back in the army, Tom. You will not rest, I know, until the war is done."

"You would not mind?"

"Have I minded to this time?" Elizabeth laughed. "No, Tom. What is in your heart to do I have accepted and always will."

Tom kissed her. "What a fortunate son of Ireland I am."

"What will you do then, Tom?" Elizabeth asked.

"Well, now," Tom said, pondering, "it seems England is again considering helping the South. If that is so—if England gets into the war—how better could I serve than by fighting the British on Irish soil and so also have a part in freeing my people?"

The more he thought of it, the more intrigued Tom Meagher became with the idea of taking an American brigade to Ireland. Before the end of June President Lincoln accepted his offer to recruit between three and four thousand volunteers. Tom called in those Irish officers of his brigade who had returned to New York and began planning.

Before actual recruiting could get under way, however, the tide of the war turned. The Confederate government, made overconfident by Lee's many victories over the large, well-equipped Federal armies, urged him to attempt a second invasion of the North. Against his better judgment, Lee obeyed the orders of President Jefferson Davis.

The Confederate army had been reinforced to its greatest strength, eighty thousand men. Leading this force, Robert E. Lee suddenly swept across the Potomac into Maryland and then into Pennsylvania. The North was near panic.

General George G. Meade had supplanted General Hooker as the commander of the Army of the Potomac. Meade led his forces, to which had been added the New York and Pennsylvania militia, against Lee. The two armies met at Gettysburg on July 1, 1863.

For three days of fierce fighting the battle raged. Lee seemed to feel that a decisive victory at Gettysburg was the one chance for success by the South. Across the valley separating the two armies, a monstrous artillery duel was waged throughout most of July 3. Gradually, the Federal artillerists stopped firing, to let the guns cool. Lee seized the momentary lull for a supreme, all-out effort.

He sent a column of fifteen thousand men under General Pickett to capture the Union batteries on Cemetery Ridge. Before they were halfway across the valley, a storm of shot and shell, a veritable hurricane, burst on the attackers furiously. The Southerners were cut down by regiments, by entire brigades, yet the remnants of the force charged on until they reached the Federal lines. It seemed as though every man in that charge felt the fate of the Confederacy depended on the assault.

The Union forces were no less desperate. As the Confederates reached the lines of the North, General Meade's men rushed from all sides to meet the attack. The battered fragments of the Southern army were defeated. They had reached their furthest penetration of Northern soil. Lee retreated to save his fragmented army.

It was not the only army success of the moment. The same day of Lee's retreat also brought news that General Ulysses S. Grant, after a brilliant maneuver and a two-month siege, had taken Vicksburg. The Mississippi was open. And there was more good news. Almost midway between those two significant Union victories, a third had taken place. General William Rosecrans had driven the rebel army of General Braxton Bragg south of the Tennessee River.

Independence Day, 1863, marked the beginning of the end of the war. It was obvious now that the South was merely marking time. And England would offer no threat to the Union. The British were too wise to join a losing cause.

"So we stop recruiting before we start," Thomas Meagher told his wife. "There will be no invasion of Ireland by an Irish Brigade."

The war progressed. The Federals, as the months went by, occupied more and more Southern territory, and it became necessary to set up military governments in those territories. They were divided into districts whose government was placed in the hands of generals, with garrisons of soldiers assigned to maintain order.

President Lincoln, searching for qualified, able men to govern these districts, men who would treat the conquered Southerners with dignity and compassion, did not overlook General Thomas Meagher. He appointed

Meagher to serve in the Provisional Division of the Army of the Tennessee. On December 23, 1863, Lincoln cancelled Meagher's resignation as brigadier general in the United States Army.

Tom Meagher reported to Major General James B. Steedman at Chattanooga. When Steedman was ordered to join Major General George Thomas at Nashville, Meagher took over active command of the district as acting major general, responsible for two regiments of cavalry, twelve thousand infantrymen, several battalions of field artillery and defense of the strong fortifications at the great bend in the Tennessee River.

It was an awesome, dangerous responsibility. The district, resenting the occupation, was overrun with guerrillas. These had to be dealt with strongly, but fairly, when caught violating any of the restrictions imposed by the occupation. And he had to maintain a steady flow of supplies to General Steedman at Nashville, over a hundred miles away.

The area he commanded, called the District of the Etowah, was extensive, covering some three hundred miles of railroad and two hundred miles of river communication. Isolated from other portions of the Federal Army, Meagher had to make do as best he could. He maintained protection of the railroad and telegraph to Knoxville, Tennessee, and Dalton, Georgia, and the steamboat transportation on the Tennessee River. Using the utmost in tact and diplomacy, he was able to keep order throughout his district without incurring the enmity of the conquered peoples in the area.

After seven weeks General Steedman returned to relieve Meagher, and Tom was ordered to join Major General William Tecumseh Sherman in Georgia. This posed
another agonizing problem for Meagher.

In July Sherman had taken Atlanta. In November he
burned it to the ground and began his March to the Sea.
His men treated the march as a great picnic, foraging
freely and destroying much property as they headed south,
singing "John Brown's Body."

Though Sherman's harshness was shortening the war,
Thomas Meagher felt himself horrified by the devastation. He had witnessed his friends and neighbors being
evicted from their homes in Ireland, had been nauseated
by the burning and looting. He had seen a house needlessly burned at the first battle of Bull Run and had de-
nounced the "ruffians" whose "scurvy and malignant"
hands had set the fire.

He had no taste for the wanton destruction of houses
and property, of cattle and cornfields. "The Irish Brigade
went out to fight the armed enemies of the Republic,"
he told his aide, "and not to cast the women, children and
aged men of the losing states naked and hungry on the
world."

"But you are to command a large unit of troops under
Sherman," the aide said. "And you asked for a return to
active service."

"I want to lead soldiers against soldiers," he said.
"Fighting soldiers is one thing, but to lead men against
women, children and old people—it is against all I know."

In the middle of January 1865 General Thomas Francis Meagher again resigned his commission in the army and returned to New York. The war, to all intents and purposes already over, did come to an end less than two months later. Robert E. Lee surrendered at Appomattox on April 9. Five days later, April 14, 1865, John Wilkes Booth, a passionate and half-mad sympathizer with the South, slipped into President Lincoln's box at Ford's Theatre in Washington, and shot the President.

Thomas Meagher, at his home on East Twenty-third Street in New York, was entertaining his friend Daniel Devlin when he first heard news of the assassination. His respect and admiration for Lincoln matched that of his affection for his "brave boys" of the Irish Brigade.

"Terrible! Terrible!" he said to Devlin. "What a waste!"

"Could Booth have hoped to help the South by such an act?" Devlin asked.

Meagher shook his head. "If Booth loved the South," he said, "he hurt it by his rashness in the worst possible way. Lincoln was a moderate man. He would have been willing to make any concession to reunite the torn parts of the Republic."

"He had already begun the work of reconstruction, according to the papers," Devlin put in.

"Actually the state of Tennessee had already been re-admitted on generous terms," Meagher added. "His death brings the more radical Republicans into control. Other states will not find it so easy to rejoin."

"But the new President, Andrew Johnson, is both a Democrat and a Southerner," Devlin said.

"He is a leader without a party," Meagher pointed out. "The Republicans control the Senate and House, and will give Johnson no peace. As the only Southern Senator who remained loyal to the Union, nothing he does will please the South either." He paused a moment, then added: "If there were only some way I could help!"

Although unaware of it at the moment, Thomas Meagher was destined to help his country further. President Andrew Johnson was anxious to take advantage of his talents.

Three months after Lincoln's death, on a July afternoon, Tom leaned against the mantelpiece in his living room reading a letter delivered that day. It was from his son across the Atlantic, in Waterford.

"Look," he said to Elizabeth, handing her a photograph enclosed with the letter. "Isn't he a strapping lad for ten years, this third Thomas Meagher?"

His wife looked long at the picture, her eyes watering. "Every bit his father's son," she said finally. "Should he not be with us here, Thomas?"

"We shall send for him and—"

Tom's words were cut short by an insistent rapping on the door. Elizabeth went to answer and returned quickly with an official letter that had been hand delivered.

"From Washington," she said, handing Tom the letter. "The office of the President."

Tom quickly opened the communication, his eyes brightening as he read. Elizabeth immediately realized the nature of its contents.

"Oh, no!" she gasped.

"My darling," Tom said. "It is, yes! President Johnson asked if I will accept an appointment as Secretary of the new Montana Territory."

"Montana!" Elizabeth echoed. "But that is thousands of miles from New York. And you will leave me again, God alone knows for how long!"

"Not for long, my darling," Tom said. "Before spring is far along, you shall join me."

"But must you accept, Tom?" Elizabeth persisted. "Montana is not only faraway, but I have read it is wild and dangerous. The Indians make so much trouble."

"Do you fear to follow me?" Tom asked jokingly.

Elizabeth Meagher's eyes darted fire. "You know better, Thomas!" she said. "It is you I fear for, going out there alone. By the time I arrive you will have quieted the wildness"—she paused—"or you will be dead!" She burst into tears.

Tom drew his wife close and kissed her hair. "You make so much of nothing," he said. "I can as easily die here in New York, this very day! Don't you remember the battles I came through unmarked?"

Nothing more was said. Thomas Meagher prepared to start west, to serve again his adopted country.

XII
DARK AND
STORMY REST

Montana had been organized as a separate territory just the year before Thomas Meagher was appointed territorial secretary, formed of two areas split by the continental divide. The eastern, and larger area, had become part of the United States in 1803, having been included in the Louisiana Purchase. The smaller, western section had been part of the Oregon country claimed by Great Britain until a treaty in 1846 gave the United States sole ownership of all land below the 49th degree of latitude, except the southern tip of Vancouver Island.

In common with most of the Northwest, Montana was in constant turmoil, seemingly from the time of Lewis and Clark. A hunting ground for Indians and rich in furs, it had been shattered by the coming of the white man, as had every territory from the Atlantic to the Pacific.

The many tribes of the Salish Indians, called the Flatheads, roamed the entire Northwest. These included the

168

Puyallup, Spokan, Squamish, Snohomish and Okinagan. As trade developed and other tribes were brought in by the fur companies, they were driven back into Washington, Oregon and British Columbia.

The discovery of gold in the 1850s and 1860s precipitated more Indian trouble. Prospectors in the Black Hills drove the Sioux west into Montana. Those in Idaho pushed the Nez Perce east about the same time. In 1863 gold was found in southwest Montana, at Alder Gulch, in the foothills of the Tobacco Root Mountains.

Sidney Edgerton had been appointed first governor of Montana in 1864. The seat of government was Virginia City, though Last Chance Gulch, later to become Helena, Montana's capital, had already been settled. It was to Governor Edgerton that Thomas Meagher was to report as secretary of the territory.

Tom left New York the second week in July, going most of the distance to Chicago by railroad. From that point on, to St. Paul, then across South Dakota and most of what is now the state of Montana, he made the trip by stagecoach. It was a rough journey, slow, tedious and dangerous. Leaving St. Paul, Minnesota, on July 27, he did not arrive in Virginia City, Montana, until October 6.

Again and again the various coaches on which he rode withstood swooping bands of Indians and occasional bandit raids. As the miles passed, Tom could not shake a premonition that he might not reach his destination, certainly that he might never again see New York.

A momentarily disturbing surprise awaited him in

Virginia City. Governor Edgerton, who had been appointed by Lincoln, had resigned soon after Andrew Johnson took office, and immediately set off for his home in Ohio. Since his successor had not arrived, the duties of acting governor fell to Secretary Thomas Meagher.

There were countless difficulties to overcome at the start. Tom was more soldier than politician. He knew only one course—what his mind told him was the right. Never had he subscribed to compromise.

From the beginning men with political aspirations, men greedily demanding the best locations for business or homestead, hemmed him in. And, though the war was over, it was still being fought on the streets and in the saloons. Many Southerners had migrated west after loss of their homes. Many still held to their old convictions.

Tom went at his duties in the only way he knew, with firmness and courage to do what he thought best once he had made a decision. As young as the territory was, it was nonetheless already gripped by partisan politics. Since Thomas Meagher had been appointed by a Democrat, and a Southerner to boot, the politicians who quickly found they could not control him worked secretly to abuse him and intrigue against anything he proposed for the good of Montana.

Immediately after assuming his office, he found a need for supplies and money to run the office. His first official act as acting governor was to call the legislature into session to provide the funds needed. His enemies wasted no time in challenging his constitutional right to assemble the legislature.

At first Tom was not sure that he had the power. Here, his experience as a lawyer aided him. He made a search for precedents. Another great soldier, one of Scotch-Irish descent, had paved the way for him in 1821.

"Here it is!" he cried out jubilantly to his assistant. "Andrew Jackson, when he was military governor of the territory of Florida, took such a responsibility!"

He called the legislature into session, defended his action in a brilliant speech which served as his message to the assembly and had his way. He accomplished his aims despite a concerted effort against him by Republican politicians who had ambitions to rule the territory.

As the months passed, Meagher was in constant conflict with those dissidents, who made every possible attempt to control his decisions. He did not yield in his determination to govern for the people and in favor of their interests.

Hamstrung to a great extent by the agitation against him, he succeeded more than a little in establishing a sound, fair government in Montana. As his successes mounted, so did his popularity among the citizens of the territory, despite the relentless enmity of what he termed the "malignant hostility of the more conspicuous and dictatorial of the Republican party."

The antagonism did not cease. Failing to disturb Meagher with open dissent and attacks in the legislature, his enemies resorted to innuendoes aimed at tarnishing his image as a loyal American. His political enemies spread rumors that he was overly friendly to the South and openly favored the interests of Southern residents in the Montana Territory.

For the most part Tom ignored the demeaning slanders. His only reference, and it was indirect, was made during a stirring speech at the Democratic convention at Helena, February 21, 1866. "On the battlefield, which they had heroically held for four tempestuous years," he said, "the soldiers of the South lowered their colors and sheathed their swords. The spirit in which they surrendered, as well as the spirit with which they fought, entitled them to respect, honorable consideration and the frank confidence of their adversaries, and the generosity of the colossal power to which they had been forced to capitulate."

There were times in those early months of his new assignment when the aggravations and the pressures brought the thought of resignation. He would contemplate the happiness and peace of a return to New York and Elizabeth. That would have been inconsistent with Tom Meagher's character, and finally he determined to continue the fight. He wrote his wife and made arrangements for her to join him in the West.

Once he received word from Elizabeth that she was on her way, that she would go from New York to St. Louis and there board a steamer that would bring her up the Missouri River to Montana, Tom went at his duties with renewed vigor. He had insisted, in his letter, that she not take the same route as he had. It was far too tiring and dangerous. Though the trip from St. Louis might take longer, it would be safer, more relaxing.

It was early spring, 1866, when Elizabeth Meagher left New York. In May she boarded the steamer *Ontario* at St. Louis, bound for Fort Benton in northern Montana, on the Missouri, some two hundred miles from Virginia City. Since the Missouri was unnavigable beyond Fort Benton, Tom would meet her there.

With every turn of the stagecoach wheels on the way to Fort Benton, Thomas Meagher became more impatient. Less than a year had passed since he left Elizabeth in New York, but it seemed like an eternity. He was exuberant, thinking of the new life ahead for both of them. There was so much opportunity in the American West, still raw and wild but fast growing. With Elizabeth at his side, what couldn't he do! With her beside him, cheering him, encouraging him, the possibilities were limitless.

It would not be long before Montana achieved statehood. He might run for governor, possibly a Senate seat, which would take him to Washington. Or, perhaps, merely the practice of law and an easy comfortable life in the shadow of the Rocky Mountains.

The stagecoach reached Fort Benton before the *Ontario*. Tom watched the ship steaming slowly up the Missouri, unable to restrain his impatience. As it came alongside, he did not wait for the lines to be secured, but leaped from the wharf to the ship's deck. Elizabeth, talking to John Doran, the captain, had not seen him.

Tom clasped her from behind and spun her around, holding her close.

"My darling! My darling!" he exclaimed breathlessly. "At long last!"

"Thomas Meagher!" Elizabeth cried out, her eyes welling with tears. "What will the good captain think! Why, never on your return from battle were you so, so—"

She drew away from him and looked up into his eyes. She kissed Tom gently on the cheek, then turned him toward the captain, standing by with a grin.

"Captain Doran," she said, "this wild man is my husband, Thomas Meagher, if you have not already suspected. Tom, this is Captain John Doran."

"Doran!" Tom exclaimed. "With such a name he's as Irish as Donegal wool!" He took Captain Doran's hand and shook it vigorously.

"There is so much to thank Captain Doran for," Elizabeth said.

"Nonsense," John Doran said. "Could I have done less for the wife of so great a man?" As Tom started to protest, Doran went on. "Of course I knew of Thomas Meagher," he said. "What Irishman doesn't?"

"I shall not forget your kindness to my wife, John Doran," Tom said as they prepared to leave the ship. "Should you come to Helena or Virginia City, you must be our honored guest."

Captain Doran shook Tom's hand warmly. "At Fort Benton, should my ship be in port, let me not hear that Thomas Meagher has taken quarters at a hotel," he said. Turning to Elizabeth, he added: "It has been my great pleasure, Mrs. Meagher. I wish you well."

As the months flew by, Thomas Meagher was happier than ever before in his life, despite the continued aggravations of his political enemies. For the first time since their marriage, he and Elizabeth were together for more than a few weeks at one time. With her at his side he began to enjoy the beauties and the challenges of life on the frontier.

Whenever his administrative duties as acting governor would allow, Tom would take Elizabeth into the Montana country, fanning out in a different direction each time from Virginia City. They marveled at the grandeur of the Rockies, rising high wherever they turned, it seemed. They would picnic beside one of the many lakes. He showed her the beginnings of the mighty Missouri River, formed by the joining of the Jefferson, Madison and Gallatin Rivers at Three Forks, midway between Virginia City and Helena.

Elizabeth loved Helena, situated so beautifully in the hollow of Prickly Pear Valley and surrounded by green-crested hills and tall, lofty mountains, with Mount Helena itself piercing the sky as a backdrop for the village.

"This is so different from life in New York," she said to Tom. "Perhaps one day we may live here."

"You must be sneaking a look into my private letters," Tom said jokingly. "Already there is talk that Helena will be the capital of the territory."

"But what a strange name for the main street of Helena," she exclaimed as they walked down Last Chance Gulch.

"Last Chance Gulch was the name of the village established on this spot," Tom pointed out. "When the vil-

lage name was changed to Helena, they kept the name
as that of the principal street. No Broadway or Fifth
Avenue, is it, but one day—who knows?"

"Many years, more likely," Elizabeth commented.

"Perhaps not. Already plans are being made for the
Northern Pacific Railroad to come into Helena."

This mushrooming growth of Montana, and all the
West for that matter, was not without its troublesome
and tragic side effects. The westward push of the white
man drove tribe after tribe of Indians from lands they
had occupied for centuries. Many of the tribes, unable
to understand the frantic grabbing of their lands, refused
to recognize land concessions made to the United States
Government by the treaty of 1863.

The year of 1866 was called "the bloody year on the
plains." About the time Elizabeth Meagher arrived in
Montana, Chief Red Cloud, a Sioux war chief, had led a
detachment of soldiers into an ambush in Wyoming, just
to the south. The soldiers, trying to keep open a road to
the Montana gold mines, were slaughtered.

In eastern Montana, along the Big Horn and the Little
Big Horn, another Sioux chief, Sitting Bull, dared the
army to take him. "The Great Spirit made me an Indian,
but he did not make me a reservation Indian," he chal-
lenged. Holing up in the Bad Lands, he made sudden
sorties west to harass settlers in Wyoming and Montana,
burning, killing and stealing in an effort to drive the
white man away.

In Montana, government agents offered to buy Indian
land from Old Joseph, the Nez Perce chief and father of

the future Chief Joseph. He refused, telling the agents: "Inside this boundary all our people were born. It circles the graves of our fathers. Let the white man take the land outside."

Thomas Meagher sympathized with the Indians. In his own Ireland he had seen how the British confiscated Irish land and ground the people into subjection. It seemed to him that the situation here was little different. A people was being ejected from its time-held lands and profiteers were carving themselves an empire from the mountain retreats of a once-proud race.

Yet, as acting governor of the territory of Montana, he had a duty to protect the citizens under his charge. And he had no militia in the territory.

"The Indians have again attacked Fort Benton," his assistant told him in greeting one morning. "What can we do?"

Thomas Meagher shook his head. "What can we do?" he said. "We must call for volunteers." He stood a moment thinking, then laughed.

His assistant gave him a quizzical look. It was hardly a laughing matter. Tom, noticing the man's puzzlement, clapped him on the back.

"I was just thinking," he said. His never failing good humor, even in moments of trouble or danger, had asserted itself with a thought. "Here I am. I am commander-in-chief, not of an invincible but of an *invisible* militia." He laughed again. This time his assistant joined in.

Meagher issued a call for volunteers and was surprised

by the quick response. There was yet another vital problem. Supplies and equipment were necessary to arm the volunteers. There were none at hand.

"I'm going to have to leave you, my darling," he told Elizabeth one morning in late June, 1867. "But it will be only for three or four days."

"I know, dear," she said. "You are going to Fort Benton."

Tom frowned. "How do you know this?" he asked. He had said nothing to anyone as yet.

"You were most worried last night," Elizabeth said. "And you do talk in your sleep. But do be careful, Thomas. I am afraid for you. The Indians and all—"

"And you don't fear for yourself?" he asked, and smiled. "But you will be safe here. And so will I, never fear."

Tom, with twelve men, left for Fort Benton on horseback. They rode furiously under a blistering sun, arriving in Fort Benton on June 29. Feeling ill, he went into the backroom of the J. G. Baker store, where he was to pick up provisions, to rest. He had been sitting reading a newspaper for perhaps ten minutes when he heard someone walk into the room. It was John Doran, captain of the steamer which had brought Elizabeth Meagher to Montana.

"Governor Meagher!" Doran exclaimed. "How lucky that I tired of fishing!" He explained that he had arrived that afternoon on his steamer, the *G. A. Thompson,* and after anchoring did a little fishing. "It must have been you leading the twelve horsemen I saw from the deck," he added. "How is Mrs. Meagher?"

"Well and happy with Montana," Tom told Doran.

Doran looked long at Tom's face. "You don't look well, Governor," he said. "Why are you here?"

Tom explained his mission. He also told Doran that he had been taken sick on the way and was laid up for two days at Sun River, a few miles west.

"When I arrived here, I found the arms and equipment I need were not at Fort Benton, but at Camp Cook. I must go there tomorrow."

"Governor," Doran said, "it is nearing dinner time. I insist that you come aboard the *Thompson* for dinner. Where are you staying in Fort Benton?"

"I had made no arrangements as yet," Tom admitted.

"Then you must stay on the *Thompson*. There is a very comfortable berth you will honor me by using."

Tom accepted both the dinner invitation and the request to spend the night aboard the steamer. After dinner Doran suggested they sit on deck.

"It's a most pleasant evening," he said. "We should enjoy the quiet and some good cigars."

They sat on deck puffing their cigars, the night balmy, the sky overhead dark and starless. Tom Meagher's eyes seemed riveted on the rushing waters of the Missouri river below. At Fort Benton the current was some nine miles an hour.

John Doran felt certain that Meagher was still ill. He seemed feverish, answering only in monosyllables when spoken to. Most of the time the man seemed faraway. Now and then his eyes would dart this way and that, then fix themselves on the torrent of water below.

Suddenly Meagher looked up and out over Fort Benton. "John!" he exclaimed. "They threaten my life in that town!"

"Nonsense, Governor!" Doran said quietly. "Why should you think that? Everybody in the territory loves you."

"No!" Meagher snapped. "While we were coming to the boat, I heard some men say, 'There he goes.'"

"It was probably someone just recognizing you as the governor, and meant nothing by it."

Meagher said nothing further for a moment. "John, are you armed?" he asked finally.

"Of course," Doran told him. "Almost everyone is armed out here, you know."

"Let me see your guns."

John Doran brought Meagher two navy revolvers. Tom took them and examined them to see if they were loaded. Finding they were, he handed them back to Doran.

Meagher lapsed into silence again. They sat there on deck, neither saying a word for another five minutes. Finally Doran spoke.

"Governor, you are very tired," he said. "Wouldn't you like to go to your berth. Rest and sleep is what you need."

Meagher agreed silently and followed John Doran to the cabin set aside for his use. He removed his coat and lay on the lower berth, still without a word. Doran drew a blanket over Meagher and turned to leave.

"Don't leave me, John!" Meagher called out. "I tell you I'm not safe."

"There's nothing to worry about, Governor," Doran

assured him. "I'll only be a few minutes. Then I'll return and sleep here in the upper berth if it will reassure you."

Doran pulled the door to the cabin shut and went down to the lower deck. He had taken but a few steps from the stairway when he heard a splash in the dark waters of the Missouri. In another second the cry "man overboard!" tore through the night air.

Doran rushed toward the rail as his engineer came bounding down the steps. "Johnny, it's your friend!" the engineer shouted. "It's Governor Meagher!"

There was a broken section in the deck rail, Doran quickly noticed. Looking into the torrential waters he realized that jumping in was useless. It would mean almost certain death. In the darkness he could see no sign of Thomas Meagher.

Was it the broken rail? Doran wondered. Then, recalling the odd behavior and Thomas Meagher's obsessive fear, the thought of possible suicide came to Doran's mind. That was impossible, he decided. He was so great a man and with so much to live for!

Calling to the deckhands to follow him, Doran leaped from the ship to the wharf and ran down the shore. Somewhere out there in the dark water was the man he respected so highly. He peered out trying to sight a thrashing body. Suddenly he heard first one, then a second, agonized cry.

Doran waved to his men to follow and rushed into the wheelhouse of the steamer *Guidon,* anchored close by. He and the men lowered themselves hip deep in the water while some of the crew of the *Guidon* threw out ropes and boards. They worked through the night and into daylight with no success.

In the morning cannons were fired and the river was dragged. They searched the shores and islands nearby. There was no sign of Thomas Meagher's body.

"The river below is dotted with innumerable small islands," John Doran explained later. "The activity of hostile Indians prevented us from exploring the ones farthest down. No doubt the body of the gallant but unfortunate general was washed ashore on one of them."

Thomas Meagher's body was never found.

EPILOGUE

So Thomas Francis Meagher—rebel, patriot, humanitarian—died, his final battle a vain struggle against the turbulent waters of the Missouri.

Some might ask why a compassionate Providence might not have had him fall on a battlefield, with either or both of the two flags he loved waving over him; why his grave might have been, not the murky waters of a Western stream, but rather the friendly green turf of an Irish hillside. His lifelong friend, Richard O'Gorman, gave the answer in his eulogy to Meagher in New York the night of August 14, 1867: "God knows best how and where and when we are to die."

From his boyhood a fighter for the rights of the common man, Thomas Meagher was a courageous idealist, always saying what he believed. The lives of few other men in all the history of the world were more changed, more checkered, more distorted and lacerated by the swirls of a capricious fate. Yet he bore all that came with an abiding confidence in justice, and a humor that belied the aches of his heart.

The Ireland which gave him birth reveres him. The America which he took as his own honors him. In America, as he had on the green hills and plains of Erin, he asked no man to a danger he would not himself face. He

183

gave all, lost all for Ireland. He risked all as a loyal soldier for America and died in her service. Lord Byron's words on the death of Richard Brinsley Sheridan make an apt memorial to Thomas Francis Meagher:

E'en as the tenderness that hour distills,
When summer's day declines along the hills;
So feels the fullness of the heart and eyes,
When all of Genius that can perish—dies.

AUTHOR'S NOTE

Many minds, many hearts and many hands helped in the writing of this story of Thomas Meagher, completed, it is hoped, with some measure of justice to his character and his varied, exciting life. Research and background review was necessarily extensive.

The author acknowledges with thanks the invaluable assistance of the many to whom he owes a debt of gratitude.

Edward McDowell Moore, Jr., of the New York office of Kenyon and Eckhardt, checked New York's American-Irish Historical Society for pertinent material available nowhere else. Two good friends in Detroit, both bibliophiles—Peter J. Harris, English expatriate and a Civil War buff, and Don Fox, with Irish expertise—were leaned on continually.

Special thanks is due to Judi Merlo, man's most efficient secretary in the writer's opinion, for typing help far beyond her normal work load. My gratitude also to Sean Brown and Henry Brenkus for varied assistance without which the book could not have been written. And let me not forget my daughter Lynda for her countless visits to the Detroit Public Library.

SUGGESTED FURTHER READINGS

The following provide further reading on the life of Thomas Francis Meagher, all used in varying degrees in researching this book:

Memoirs of Gen. Thomas Francis Meagher, by Michael Cavanaugh. Worcester, Mass., Messenger Press, 1892.

Life of General Meagher, by Capt. W. F. Lyons. New York, D. & J. Sadlier & Co., 1870.

Thomas Francis Meagher—An Irish Revolutionary in America, by Robert G. Athern. Boulder, Colo., University of Colorado Press, 1949.

Battles and Leaders of the Civil War. New York, Thomas Yoseloff, Inc., 1956.

INDEX

ABOUT THE AUTHOR

David J. Abodaher was born in Streator, Illinois, but moved with his family at the age of five to Detroit, Michigan, where he has lived most of his life. He attended Detroit parochial schools, with his college years spent at the University of Detroit and Notre Dame, paying his own way through free-lance writing.

His first efforts, written and sold in his late teens, were mystery, western and sports pulp fiction, followed by radio dramas. Leaving Notre Dame after the first semester of his senior year, he entered the broadcasting field full time, writing dramatic scripts and documentaries and announcing sports. He also worked as producer and program director at radio stations in Detroit, Cincinnati, Oklahoma City and Kalamazoo.

During World War II he served in the U.S. Army Signal Corps and when the war was over, he returned to Detroit and entered the field of advertising. Appointed Radio Director of his agency, he found himself back in the broadcast area, writing commercial spots and doing on-the-air assignments in sports.

Moving into business for himself as a creator and producer of radio and television features, he also put his interest and knowledge of photography to work, writing, directing and producing commercial and public-service motion pictures. Special writing and photography assignments for the Ford Motor Company led him back into advertising with the Ford agency, the J. Walter Thompson Company, and then to Kenyon & Eckhardt Inc.

Mr. Abodaher is an American history buff and the author of several biographies for young people. His hobby, other than photography, is reading history. He has one daughter, Linda.